Penguin

Eugén

Arnold S
became a
of Roeh;

Penguin Masterstudies

Honoré de Balzac

Eugénie Grandet

Arnold Saxton

Penguin Books

Penguin Books Ltd, Harmondsworth, Middlesex, England
Viking Penguin Inc., 40 West 23rd Street, New York, New York 10010, U.S.A.
Penguin Books Australia Ltd, Ringwood, Victoria, Australia
Penguin Books Canada Limited, 2801 John Street, Markham, Ontario, Canada L3R 1B4
Penguin Books (N.Z.) Ltd, 182–190 Wairau Road, Auckland 10, New Zealand

First published 1987

Made and printed in Great Britain by
Richard Clay (The Chaucer Press) Ltd, Bungay, Suffolk
Filmset in Monophoto Times

Contents

1   Balzac and his Novel

Honoré de Balzac, 1799–1850

Honoré de Balzac was born in Tours, the eldest of four children. Originally from the south-west of France, as the ending -*ac* indicates, the Balzacs were of peasant origin, rising towards the middle classes. Bernard-François Balzac, Honoré's father, was a notable example of this evolution, since he became active in the administration of the French army at a glorious period of its history, under Napoleon.

There seems to have been little overt affection between the parents and their children, or indeed between the parents themselves (the youngest son, Henri, born in 1807, was almost certainly fathered by a friend of the family), and Honoré's emotional attachments were with his two sisters Laure (born 1800) and Laurence (born 1802). Placed in a boarding-school at an early age, Honoré spent years of loneliness, recalled in some of his fiction, notably in *Le Lys dans la vallée*.

None the less, he developed an abiding love of the landscape of Touraine, that middle section of the valley of the Loire centred on the old city of Tours, which he used as a setting for a number of his works, including *Le Lys dans la vallée* and the short novella *Le Curé de Tours*. He absorbed a great store of knowledge about provincial society, its attitudes and prejudices, its priorities and weaknesses, which he readily attributed to other regions of France   to Angoulême in *Les Illusions perdues*, for example.

Although Balzac's roots lie in the provincial society of the Napoleonic era, his family moved to Paris in 1814. He completed his studies in 1819 and set up in his own lodgings, determined to conquer the world of letters and, above all, the theatre. Unfortunately, his tragedy *Cromwell* received an icy reception when he read it to his family, and he reluctantly abandoned the drama for the worlds of journalism and fiction.

Over the next ten years Balzac published many pot-boiling novels, or more properly novelettes, using pseudonyms such as 'Lord R'Hoone' (an anagram of Honoré), and sometimes working with a collaborator. These were his 'galley years', to borrow a term used by the composer Verdi to designate the slog of producing work to order rather than from artistic choice. Virtually unknown today, these early works nevertheless yield many interesting pre-echoes of the later, mature novels, not least of *Eugénie Grandet*.

Two events marked Balzac's twenties, and were to shape his attitudes. The first was his affaire with Laure de Berny, forty-five years old to his twenty-two, who became for him both the affectionate mother he had failed to find in his family, and the tender lover and wise friend who initiated him into the pitfalls of passion and of work. Her influence permeates all his later sexual relationships, and it was to Mme de Berny that he turned for advice until his sister, also named Laure, became his confidante.

Just before his liaison with Mme de Berny began, Balzac had seen his younger sister Laurence married against her will. (Laure had earlier contracted a happy marriage.) Laurence died in 1825 – of despair, according to Honoré. His parents. and especially his mother, were never forgiven for their part in this mismatch, and throughout his life Balzac maintained a curious love–hate relationship with his mother, who survived him by five years (his father died in 1829).

The 1820s were further marked by Balzac's entry into Parisian society as a young dandy, and – not unconnected with this – by his constant need for cash. Money was to play a dominant role in Balzac's life. He was an obsessive spender – he bought gloves by the gross   and. for one whose novels reveal an intimate and shrewd appraisal of financial transactions, he was surprisingly incompetent. The fortunes he made in later years by his writings disappeared in crackbrained schemes, dubious investments and sheer profligacy. Even at the height of his fame he was often at bay from creditors, and resorted on occasion to maintaining two or more apartments, moving from one to another in order to fend off his tradesmen.

These early years of authorship laid the foundations of his great knowledge of the mechanisms of Parisian society, the passage from garret to brilliant salon furnishing contrasts he was to exploit in the first of his Parisian masterpieces, *Le Père Goriot* (1834).

In 1829, the first novel under his own name of Honoré Balzac (the honorific 'de' was added later) appeared. This was *Les Chouans*, dealing with the attempt by forces sympathetic to the monarchy to resist the spread of republicanism in the Brittany of 1800. Strongly influenced by Scott, *Les Chouans* remains very readable, and to some extent broke new ground in applying Scott's historical methods to a period still within living memory. Next followed a series of short works, stories rather than novels, grouped as *Scènes de la vie privée*. None figures among his masterpieces, though this is perhaps the place to say that the level of Balzac's output of over ninety works is extraordinarily consistent, and that even his minor productions are marked by his personal views and his immense energy.

La Peau de chagrin, published in 1831 and described as an 'étude philosophique', is possibly the least readable of the longer early works. The plot, based on a fantasy of the granting of wishes, almost founders under a torrent of asides, long evocations of pell-mell impressions and implausible transitions. Melodrama reigned in the popular theatre of the day, and *La Peau de chagrin* follows this trend. Nevertheless, the work is important as a statement of Balzac's views on fate and free-will, on love and death, and as a portrait of a doomed 'Romantic' hero, Raphaël.

Balzac also chooses this novel to formulate his ideas on energy, both physical and psychic, which later works were to confirm as one of his major themes. The succinct formula: 'Vouloir, pouvoir, savoir' is communicated to Raphaël by a mysterious antique dealer, who explains:

Vouloir nous brûle, et *pouvoir* nous détruit, mais SAVOIR laisse notre faible organisation dans un perpetuel état de calme.

(*Wanting* burns us up, and *having our will* destroys us, but KNOWING leaves our feeble system in an everlasting state of repose.)

The interest of this notion will be evident to readers of *Eugénie Grandet*, with its twin portraits of obsession.

Again there followed several short works before *Eugénie Grandet* was published in December 1833 as part of the *Scènes de la vie privée*. In 1834 a daughter, presumed to be Balzac's child, was born to Maria du Fresnay, who became the dedicatee of the first separate edition of the work in 1839.

Balzac's career after *Eugénie Grandet* can be quickly told. He conceived the notion of a vast interlocking series of novels to depict the whole of society from the early days of the century to contemporary France. This was to bear the overall title *La Comédie humaine*, and Balzac revised all his earlier works in order to bring them under this new heading. One of the principal features was to be the recurrence of characters, who would be seen in varying degrees of importance in different works, and whose 'existence' would thereby be given density and credibility. Balzac was still adding to this series when he died – partly of overwork – in 1850. Some ten of these novels rank as European masterpieces; the others are never less than a fascinating record of the evolution of French society between 1810 and 1846.* Balzac may truly be said to have created a world, and each of these novels constitutes a world within that world.

* Each enthusiast has a list of favourite works by Balzac, but a general consensus would probably include *Le Colonel Chabert* (1832), *Eugénie Grandet* (1833), *Le Père Goriot* (1834), *Les Illusions perdues* (1837–43), *Grandeur et décadence de César Birotteau* (1837), *Splendeurs*

His private life consisted of increasing pressure to work for money, and involvement with a large number of women, one of whom, the Polish Countess Hanska, he married a few months before his death.

Balzac and the literary life of his time

It has often been said that the nineteenth century is the age of the novel. This is not to overlook the existence of masterpieces from at least as early as *Don Quixote* in the late sixteenth century, but the reader certainly feels a new urgency in the novelists of the nineteenth century after the generally leisurely pace, and sometimes cumbersome techniques, of eighteenth-century practitioners of the novelist's art. Moreover, the novel, last-born of the great literary genres, presupposes a literate public: plays can be seen, poems heard, but novels are usually read by the individual. For as long as the public was relatively limited and the cost of production high, the great age of the novel as a mass medium could not dawn. It is typical of Balzac's inquiring and energetic approach to life that, dissatisfied with the mechanics of the production of his works, he devised an improved printing-press; when existing paper proved inadequate for the requirements of the new machines, he proceeded to investigate the manufacture of paper with a view to improving that also (equally typically he lost a great deal of money in these ventures, but used the experience in *Les Illusions perdues*).

The great explosion of creative energy in the arts in France which followed the collapse of Napoleon's empire in 1815 threw up painters, musicians, sculptors and, above all, writers. The Romantic movement, already an artistic reality in other countries, was a late starter in France, and only in the 1820s can literature really be said to have shaken off the influences of older, more conservative forms. If poetry spearheaded the new writing, the novel was not far behind, and Balzac forms part of a cohort of new young writers who came to prominence before 1830.

Several of these young writers were the leading poets of the day, who were also trying their hand at drama and the novel. They saw as their immediate predecessors such writers as Benjamin Constant, whose short novel *Adolphe*, published in 1816, will be referred to later; Chateaubriand, father of French Romanticism and author of *René*, almost a pattern for future Romantic heroes; and Mme de Staël, a cosmopolitan

---

et misères des courtisanes (1838–47) and *La Cousine Bette* (1846). Other important works are *La Peau de chagrin* (1830–31), *Le Lys dans la vallée* (1835), *La Rabouilleuse* (1840–42) and *Le Cousin Pons* (1847).

writer, more influential for her treatises on literature, *De l'Allemagne* and *De la littérature*, than for her feminist novels *Corinne* and *Delphine*. With the exception of *Adolphe*, none of these is greatly admired today. The works of Balzac's contemporaries at about the time of *Eugénie Grandet* have perhaps fared better, but here too reservations must be made.

Dominating the young Romantics was Victor Hugo, some of whose novels are certainly still read. *Notre Dame de Paris* (1831) contains famous and picturesque scenes familiar to all cinemagoers, as does his much later work *Les Misérables* (1861). Alexandre Dumas, in a series of novels written during the 1840s, captured a large public with *Le Comte de Monte Cristo* (1844) and *Les Trois Mousquetaires* (1844). The young Prosper Mérimée evoked the sixteenth century with an exercise in the style of Scott, *Chronique du règne de Charles IX* (1829). All these works are still widely read, but by an unsophisticated readership. They have become works to be absorbed during adolescence, exciting, rather undemanding and not usually the object of intensive literary analysis.

Mérimée went on to produce more sophisticated works such as *Carmen* and *Colomba*, and one of his great friends emerged as the only novelist of the 1830s comparable in stature with Balzac. Stendhal (the pen-name of Henri Beyle, 1783–1847) completed only four novels, but two of these have since become accepted as pinnacles of the novelist's art: *Le Rouge et le noir* (1830) and *La Chartreuse de Parme* (1839). Very different in style and temper from Balzac, Stendhal shares Balzac's mistrust of the new society and, in *Le Rouge et le noir*, he depicts a young provincial's calculated moves up the ladders which society affords, until he is plunged back to the bottom, and finally to the condemned cell. Julien Sorel, Stendhal's hero, has emerged as the most original and most brilliantly depicted of all French fictional creations of the early nineteenth century.

Balzac was thus working among a phalanx of eager novelists all set upon capturing the ever-growing circle of readers created by the availability of cheaper books and by serialized publication. We must also be aware that there were a large number of now forgotten writers, churning out the romances and melodramas which Balzac himself had perpetrated in his youth. But *Eugénie Grandet* stands apart, both from the general production of the time, and, to a certain extent, from the mainstream of Balzac's own work. We shall now look at it in detail.

2 Some Aspects of the Novel in 1833

Anglo-Saxon readers, asked to name the most famous novelists of the first quarter of the nineteenth century, would probably cite Jane Austen and Walter Scott. The former name would have surprised readers of 1833, since her accession to the pantheon of novelists was largely a posthumous, if not indeed a twentieth-century phenomenon. Scott, however, would certainly have been approved. His novels were immensely popular, and, being prose works, they exported well. The influence of Scott pervades the European novel of the first half of the nineteenth century. The evocation of the past and of lands remote enough to be exotic (Scotland, England) corresponded to the taste of the Romantic generation for the colourful, the strange. They evoked the half-legendary world of romance, balladry and folk tale. At the same time, Scott's novels convinced by the meticulous re-creation of the historical period chosen, within the limits of scholarship available to the writer. To some degree, works such as *Quentin Durward, Old Mortality* or *The Heart of Midlothian* are documentaries of the age in which they are set. More especially, Scott presents the lives of ordinary people alongside those of historical or heroic characters, and this willingness to give prominence to the humble provides a salutary balance to the chivalrous exploits of the hero or the villainy of his enemies. The vitality of such low-life figures as Jeanie Deans (*The Heart of Midlothian*) or Old Mortality suggests that Scott was, in fact, more at ease in depicting the common people than the gentry, many of whom seem to the modern reader faceless and interchangeable.

Scott's influence on *Les Chouans* has already been noted, but his method is harnessed to the service of an almost contemporary story. Only thirty years separate the story of the Chouans from Balzac's novel about them, whereas Scott normally allowed a greater time-lag. Balzac thus takes from Scott what he judges to be useful, and depicts a situation which, though historical, is still of great contemporary influence – the young hero of *Les Chouans* reappears as a venerable national hero in one of Balzac's last works, *La Cousine Bette*, in 1846! This interest in a relatively recent past reappears in *Eugénie Grandet*, where the historical context of Grandet's fortune is briefly but (for a contemporary reader) tellingly sketched in.

More fundamentally, Scott's juxtaposition of Romantic and 'realist' elements finds its echo in Balzac. Balzac's novels, and in particular his earlier, shorter works, contemporary with *Eugénie Grandet*, reveal a taste for the *outré*, the melodramatic, the violent. Some are set in the past or in foreign countries, following the fashionable exotic taste of the time, but even the more substantial works contain scenes, particularly headlong confrontations, which seem to be survivals from earlier novels, or echoes of the popular theatre of the day. One may cite the appearance at the dead of night of the supposedly dead Colonel Chabert in the novella of that name; or in the arrest of Vautrin, revealed as a master-criminal, in the dingy boarding-house in *Le Père Goriot*. *Eugenie Grandet* contains at least one scene in this tradition: Eugénie's threat to kill herself as her father attacks Charles's 'nécessaire', and her mother cries out from her sickbed. Equally, there are Romantic elements in the characterization of Eugénie, though these are undercut by the realism of Balzac's description of her very ordinary appearance.

Most of all, the influence of Scott can be seen in the choice of a drab, outwardly quite unremarkable family as the centre of the novelist's attention. Few possibilities exist in Saumur for Romantic heroes or for passionate abandon. Yet, within the limits he has imposed on his characters, Balzac suggests that the most ordinary of lives can be touched by romance, and that the most unpromising décor can provide a Romantic setting.

However, the influence of Scott and of the more extravagant Romantic models is not predominant in *Eugénie Grandet*. Though written in the Romantic era, the novel belongs at least in part to an older French tradition, the analytical novel ('le roman d'analyse'). Springing from the doctrines propounded in the seventeenth century by the Académie Française, the classical school of writing made its greatest impact on French literature in the field of drama, where the qualities of restraint and nobility of purpose proposed by the Académie permeated the theatre of tragedy for well over a century. The Académie had further prescribed for serious drama certain rules governing the duration and place of the action, and had insisted that plots should not be over-complicated. The aim was to make the tragic drama more believable ('vraisemblable') and to concentrate the emotions of the spectator on a single situation explored in depth. The Académie was fortunate in that the seventeenth century produced two tragic dramatists of genius in Corneille and Racine, whose works ensured that the rules they obeyed were immediately seen as potentially beneficial to writers, rather than as a strait-jacket.

The novel, a new and as yet not highly regarded literary genre in the seventeenth century, was not subjected to the scrutiny of the Académie, but the pervasive influence of classical ideals was felt by its practitioners. The acknowledged masterpiece of the novel in seventeenth-century France is Mme de La Fayette's *La Princesse de Clèves*, which explores one woman's dilemma with great sensitivity. Its analytical approach to character, using events as a springboard for the ever-deepening self-knowledge of its heroine, mark *La Princesse de Clèves* as the novelistic equivalent of a tragedy by Corneille. The foundations of a tradition had been laid down, and the 'roman d'analyse' was to become a constant in the French literary tradition, stretching through Prévost's *Manon Lescaut*, Constant's *Adolphe*, embracing such longer works as Flaubert's *Madame Bovary* or Fromentin's *Dominique* in the nineteenth century, and re-emerging in the works of twentieth-century writers such as Gide, Mauriac, Colette and Duras.

Each of the novelists cited above brings to the 'roman d'analyse' his or her own contribution; the novel is an infinitely flexible genre, and some would no doubt query the word 'analytical' when applied to, say, *Madame Bovary*. The close scrutiny of a single dilemma is, however, an incontrovertible strength of the French novelistic tradition, and to that tradition *Eugénie Grandet* belongs. Balzac was always conscious of the dramatic substructure of the novel form – indeed, many of his novels were adapted for the stage during his lifetime, *Eugénie Grandet* among them; and we shall see how he has drawn upon theatrical associations in his writing. It seems highly likely that this novel has the classical drama as one of its forebears. Balzac himself writes in dramatic terms, using the word 'acteur' to define Grandet's tone of voice, or, in the phrase 'les acteurs de cette scène', to designate the Grandets and their guests. More significantly, Balzac draws a comparison between the family drama he narrates and Greek classical tragedy:

... une tragédie bourgeoise sans poison, ni poignard, ni sang répandu; mais, relativement aux acteurs, plus cruelle que tous les drames accomplis dans l'illustre famille des Atrides.

(. . . a bourgeois tragedy undignified by poison, dagger, or bloodshed, but to the protagonists more cruel than any of the tragedies endured by the members of the noble house of Atreus.)

We must, however, be aware of the popularity in Balzac's own day of the 'drame', or 'melodrame' (technically, a drama with musical accompaniment under the speech, like film background music). Balzac sometimes in *Le Père Goriot*, for example – seeks to dissociate a highly-coloured plot from unfavourable comparison with the popular, debased 'd4rames' of the day. None the less, the high classical tradition which we may perceive as underlying *Eugénie Grandet* has been touched by elements of the 'drame', notably in the violent confrontation between Eugénie and her father.

It can be seen that Balzac's novel lies at the crossroads of two traditions. Part of its interest to us today comes from the tension arising from that confrontation, and this aspect of the work will be explored in the concluding section of this study.

3   What Sort of Novel?

I have already suggested that the novel as a genre is the freest of all literary forms. Untrammelled by considerations of stage practicability or of rhyme and verse, which constrain dramatist and poet, the novelist knows no limitations on the length, content or form of his work other than those he chooses. Only the distinction between the novel proper and the longer short story or novella hints at some frontier, and even here the prime concern is with nomenclature. Balzac's output ranges from short stories, through novellas such as *Le Colonel Chabert*, to novels several hundred pages in length – indeed, *Les Illusions perdues* frequently occupies two volumes. *Eugénie Grandet* is one of the shortest of those works by Balzac which can be called, by their length, novels proper.

Within this immense freedom, the novelist must make choices. He must, for example, decide on any inner divisions he may wish to make. Here Balzac hesitated. His first published version of the novel, which appeared as Volume 1 of a four-volume set of *Scènes de la Vie de Province* in 1833, contained chapter divisions. These were removed when the novel was published separately in 1839. Most editions today, including the Garnier-Flammarion edition to which quotations and page-references in French refer (GF), and the Penguin translation (P)* correspondingly used, follow the later edition in suppressing the chapter divisions. It is of interest, however, to see how Balzac envisaged his work as falling into sections.

Each of the original chapters bore a title, as follows:

Chapter 1, 'Physionomies bourgeoises' (GF pp. 27–54, P pp. 33–69)
This covers the author's presentation of the Saumurois setting and characters, and the birthday party, up to the arrival of Charles.

Chapter 2, 'Le Cousin de Paris' (GF pp. 54–70, P pp. 69–91)
A description of Charles and his impact on the group. The events stemming from his welcome, and the letter from Grandet's brother. The family retire to bed.

---

* The translator of the Penguin edition has sometimes re-worded the French text quite radically.

Chapter 3, 'Amours de province' (GF pp. 70–101, P pp. 91–132)
Eugénie's awakening to love, her small schemes to please Charles, and
the revelation of her uncle's suicide.

Chapter 4, 'Promesses d'avare, serments d'amour' (GF pp. 101–39, P pp.
132–82)
Grandet is occupied with his financial stratagems. Eugénie and Charles
come closer together. Charles leaves for the Indies. Grandet's plans for
his brother's estate succeed.

Chapter 5, 'Chagrins de famille' (GF pp. 139–69, P pp. 182 221)
Grandet quarrels with Eugénie about her gift of the *douzain*, but, after
her long isolation, he accepts Cruchot's advice to make his peace with
her. Discovering the *nécessaire*, he precipitates a violent scene which
leads to Mme Grandet's death. Five years later Grandet also dies, Nanon
marries, but Eugénie still awaits news of Charles.

Chapter 6, 'Ainsi va le monde' (GF pp. 169–87, P pp. 221–45)
Now thirty, Eugénie lives only for her love for Charles. Eventually he
writes to announce his marriage. Eugénie marries M. de Bonfons so as
to have an agent in her plan to pay off Charles's debts. Charles realizes
too late what he has lost.

Conclusion (GF pp. 187–9, P pp. 245–8)
A rapid account of Eugénie's brief marriage and early widowing. She
still lives in Saumur.

It will be seen that the titles reflect the flow of the psychological
action, rather than the events of the story. The chapters also serve to
highlight the peculiar time-scheme of the novel, the first one in particular
containing no action at all. Balzac's decision to dispense with inner
divisions was no doubt correct, since the single thrust of the novel's
development requires no punctuation to allow the reader to get his
bearings. The action flows inexorably forward, and, indeed, on two
occasions (GF pp. 101, 187) the Garnier-Flammarion edition does not
even have a pause for a new paragraph as one former chapter merges
into the next.
A novelist faces many other, more important decisions when planning
his novel. Crucial among those relating to technique is his choice of
narrative voice. Shall he use a first-person narration, as Charlotte Brontë
did in *Jane Eyre*? Will the epistolary style of the novel-in-letters, much

favoured in the eighteenth century, be appropriate? Most novelists opt for the 'omniscient narrator' technique whereby the novelist is assumed to be telling the story, and to be privy to the thoughts and actions of any character, as it suits him. This is the solution most favoured by Balzac (he had essayed the first-person form, as a sort of extended letter from the hero of *Le Lys dans la vallée*). It enables the novelist to follow his characters, to pass from one to another without strain, to describe externals impartially and to incorporate such comments as he sees fit.

Balzac often does see fit to comment. By and large, novelists can be categorized as directive and non-directive; there are those who mediate between reader and narrative, offering moral views; those who manipulate the reader's sympathies overtly; and those who, conversely, use irony to jolt the reader's sensibilities. In English literature, George Eliot exemplifies the first of these intentions, Dickens the second, Jane Austen the last – though none uses only one sort of intervention. In French literature, Stendhal is perhaps the supreme ironist and Balzac the most notable moraliser among nineteenth-century novelists. The generation after theirs saw a reaction against authorial intervention. Flaubert, and to a lesser extent Zola, aimed to eliminate from the novel any trace of the author's personality or views. Novelists of our own day lean to one side or another, as the novel form has become ever more free.

Balzac's authorial comments range from the passing aside to the fullblown effusion, one of his chief fingerprints as a writer and one which many modern readers find unpalatable. Thus we find in the first paragraph of the novel, in the evocation of Saumur, a sentence which directs our response to the town before we even see it. Balzac opens his novel with a comparison between the melancholy aspect of provincial towns and that of cloisters, heaths or ruins, and goes on to tell us why such a comparison might be made.

Peut-être y a-t-il à la fois dans ces maisons et le silence du cloître et l'aridité des landes et les ossements des ruines. (GF p. 27)

(These houses may combine the cloister's silence with the arid desolation of the waste and the sepulchral melancholy of ruins.) (P p. 33)

Here, the novelist is directing the reader's choice of associations by providing those which he wishes to be linked with old towns like Saumur. In fact, the words 'cloître', 'landes' and 'ruines' might suggest very different qualities to some readers, but Balzac, at this crucial early stage of his novel, clearly feels that the public must be led along paths which he has already chosen. Such minor manipulations are the common coin of novel-writing, and will be encountered very frequently in *Eugénie Grandet*.

What some readers will find more intrusive is Balzac's willingness to stop the flow of narrative or analysis in order to interpose his own views on some aspect of society, of his characters' behaviour, or on moral issues in general. Thus a brief account of Nanon's history, and of her place in the Grandet household, culminating in Grandet's pitying interjection, 'Cette pauvre Nanon!', elicits from Balzac this comment:

Qui ne dira pas aussi: Pauvre Nanon! Dieu reconnaîtra ses anges aux inflexions de leurs voix et à leurs mystérieux regrets. (GF p. 42)

(Who can refrain from repeating 'Poor Nanon'? God will know his angels by the tones of their voices and the sadness hidden in their hearts.) (P p. 54)

Some readers may have other views on Nanon's dog-like devotion, finding it ridiculous or degrading. Others again may be embarrassed by Balzac's pietistic moralizing. Longer interventions include disquisitions on the mechanisms of power (GF p. 100, P p. 130), on girls in love (GF p. 119, P p. 155), on the corruptions of Paris (GF pp. 119–20, P pp. 155–6), a comparison between falling in love and being newly born (GF p. 129, P pp. 168–9), and several others. It is clear that Balzac views his authorial role as a guiding, didactic one. At the same time, these asides contribute much to the particular flavour of the novel. They allow Balzac to introduce a wider perspective in what might otherwise be seen as a localized and somewhat petty domestic drama. In particular, the author's interventions add a dimension to be found in other novels set in the provinces.

For Balzac, certain provincial settings, notably those of the Loire valley, seem to hold associations of innocence, purity, other-worldliness, which are linked for him with religious observance. Though not noticeably pious himself, Balzac remained throughout his life convinced that the monarchy and the Catholic Church provided the twin buttresses of the social edifice   he states this clearly in a preface he wrote to the *Comédie humaine*. The novel is studded with references to the rewards of the hereafter, to the saintly patience of Eugénie, and of her mother, whose dying days are explicitly contrasted with the total materialism of her husband's last interests on earth. This aspect of *Eugénie Grandet* appears in the dedication which Balzac added for the 1839 edition. 'Maria' has been identified as Mme Marie du Fresnay, who at the time of the novel's first publication was Balzac's mistress and whose daughter, born in 1834, is believed to have been his illegitimate child. These circumstances might seem to render inapposite the lofty and spiritual tone of the dedication, with its references to 'buis bénit', 'mains pieuses', etc., but the reader is thereby alerted to that element of the novel to which

19

Balzac attached importance. If the tone of the dedication may today be considered not only chaste but also smug, it may well be that those very qualities of the novel itself ensured that, of all Balzac's *œuvre*, this was the work which the nineteenth century considered   and indeed our own century considers, too – the best introduction to 'adult' reading for young people. *Eugénie Grandet* has, in fact, suffered in critical esteem as a result of its association with an adolescent public.

The novelist, in planning his work, must decide on a time-scheme and on the *locus* of the action. For *Eugénie Grandet*, the latter presents few problems. The action never moves from Saumur,* and such events as Des Grassins's negotiations over Guillaume Grandet's estate, and Charles's career in trade are evoked obliquely. The world of Saumur encloses the Grandet family, and the authenticity of the background seems assured. However, surprisingly little concrete and precisely localized detail is given about Saumur. No street or square is named – not even when Nanon is intercepted by other servants as she goes to market. When Eugénie and her mother attend mass, the church is not specified beyond being the parish church, and it would, in fact, seem that Balzac barely knew Saumur, having passed through the town in 1830. Much of the 'characteristic' architecture and the local customs apply to Touraine as much as to Anjou, the region round Saumur, and evidence from the manuscript shows that, on occasion, Balzac had thought first of his beloved Touraine. For example, the word 'frippe'. used by Nanon, now carries an explanation beginning 'En Anjou . . .'. The original manuscript reads: 'En Touraine et en Anjou . . .'. Indications of this kind can be found in the Pléiade edition of the *Comédie humaine* (volume 3), where the scholarly notes of a team of Balzac specialists enlighten many corners of the text.

It appears, then, that Balzac's Saumur is something of a myth. Why not locate the novel openly in, say, Tours, or Blois? No doubt a town further downstream was needed to make Grandet's dealings with the shipyards at Nantes more plausible, and it may have been prudent to avoid too close an identification with known skinflints in Tours. The important thing is that Balzac's picture of a small town convinces us, and we do not need to read the novel with a street-map of Saumur to hand.

The matter of chronology is rather less simple. The novelist may play tricks with time, using flashback, flashforward, or simultaneous presentation of events set far apart; he may wish time to be elastic, so that a

---

* The only exceptions being the glimpse of Charles writing his letter to Eugénie, and his meeting with de Bonfons.

short sequence of events occupies more pages than a longer one. Novelists commonly use all these devices, and others, but Balzac in *Eugénie Grandet* follows a simple chronological sequence for most of the time. The early pages convey a great deal of essential information about the past of Félix Grandet, yet very little about his wife and none about his daughter. Indeed, we learn more about Charles's youth in a retrospective paragraph at the time of his arrival on the scene than we ever know about Eugénie's life before that fateful evening. From that first scene at her birthday gathering, Balzac allows the story to unreel strictly chronologically, except for the *hors-texte* showing how Grandet's plans for coping with his brother's creditors work out in practice, and the fate of M. des Grassins in Paris. This flashforward can be justified in that it follows closely on Grandet's manoeuvrings in Saumur and at the same time answers the reader's curiosity, leaving Balzac free to concentrate on family matters in Saumur. We are also vaguely aware that the love interest and the money plot are progressing simultaneously without this being obtrusive.

More startling than this minor manipulation of the strict order of events is Balzac's sleight-of-hand with the lapse of time in the novel. Far from being smooth, the coverage of events is highly selective. Over a period of seven or eight years Balzac selects only a few days, leaving vast gaps during which either nothing is reported, or the plot advances only in the most general terms – for example, in Balzac's handling of the last weeks (or is it months?) of Grandet's life. The reader is aware of a progressive decline, examples are given of the old man's sayings or commands, but only the deathbed itself is given a specific treatment, with the blasphemous grasping for the gilt crucifix and the dying man's injunctions to Eugénie.

Moreover, the different highlighted events occupy very varied stretches of the novel. Most obviously, over half the book is devoted to events which occur between the arrival of the local worthies on Eugénie's birthday and the two days that follow. The action then becomes less precise until Charles's departure and, after a gap of several weeks, resumes on New Year's Day. After Eugénie's sequestration, a new crisis point comes with Grandet's apparent change of heart in releasing her, and his discovery of the 'nécessaire'. The next action scene is that of the old man's death, for Mme Grandet's deathbed is not in fact dealt with in precise terms.

Thus Balzac has almost abused the novelist's control over time, slowing down, eliding and accelerating as he pleases. The justification lies in the fact that his method is so successful. How many, reading the work for the first time, are aware of its curious layout, and how many resent such care being lavished on those crucial few days of crisis in Charles's affairs?

One area of the novel which may elicit a hostile response from the reader is Balzac's slow and careful setting of the action in place and period. This particular decision by the novelist deserves separate consideration.

4 The Introduction to the Action

Today's reader may feel some impatience with the slow opening of *Eugénie Grandet*. The novelistic conventions of our own day require the author to engage the reader's attention and to promote his involvement with the characters in the opening paragraphs. It is no accident that Jane Austen, whose openings are strikingly 'modern', is read more widely today than Scott, who prefers a more leisurely style. Nor is Balzac's slowly unfolding introduction unique to *Eugénie Grandet* – the first pages of *Le Père Goriot*, written a year later, display a similar preoccupation with setting rather than with character, and the relatively brisk start of the earlier *La Peau de chagrin* contains many reflective paragraphs in the description of events which form its opening episode.

Balzac chooses, of course, to begin in this way. He evidently views his leisurely, descriptive approach as essential to the deeper implications of his story.

As in *Le Père Goriot*, he is concerned to evoke a place. Saumur represents that provincial society apparently still untouched by the tremendous events which had shaken France during Grandet's lifetime. The reader is asked to saunter down the main street and to let his gaze probe, camera-like, into the closed houses which also serve as shops. The novelist acts as guide, revealing that appearances can be deceptive, and that a bare interior and an apparent dearth of merchandise may conceal great wealth.

Les échantillons consistent en deux ou trois baquets pleins de sel et de morue, en quelques paquets de toile à voile, des cordages, du laiton pendu aux solives du plancher, des cercles le long des murs, ou quelques pièces de drap sur des rayons. (GF p. 28)

(The samples displayed consist of two or three tubs of salt and salt codfish, or a few bales of sailcloth or coils of rope, copper wire hanging from the rafters, cask hoops along the walls, or some lengths of cloth on the shelves.) (P p. 35)

Vous verrez un marchand de merrain assis à sa porte et qui tourne ses pouces en causant avec un voisin, il ne possède en apparence que de mauvaises planches à bouteilles et deux ou trois paquets de lattes; mais sur le port son chantier plein fournit tous les tonneliers de l'Anjou; il sait, à une planche près, combien il *peut* de tonneaux si la récolte est bonne. (GF pp. 28–9)

(You will see a dealer in barrel staves sitting at his door twiddling his thumbs as he gossips with a neighbour: to all appearances he possesses nothing more than some rickety bottle racks and two or three bundles of laths, yet his well-stocked timber-yard on the quay supplies all the coopers in Anjou. He knows, to a stave, how many casks he can *do* for you, if the vintage is good.) (P p. 35)

This anonymous dealer, these uninviting interiors, serve the obvious end of preparing the reader for the character of Grandet and of his household. We must not lose sight of these early pages when considering the events of the story. They hint at a generalization of what might otherwise be seen as an exceptional, aberrant, even implausible premise – that Eugénie has no idea of her father's wealth.

However, these early pages, in which the old town is evoked, convey far more than a dismal picture of graceless living. Balzac's attitude to Saumur has undertones which may surprise us unless we remain aware of his love of the Loire valley and unless we recall how much of Touraine there is in this Angevin setting. Elsewhere in his novels the provinces receive scant sympathy. Even so important a local centre as Angoulême in *Les Illusions perdues* is dismissed finally as hopelessly retrograde, and its finest local talent seems shabby and provincial when exposed to the spotlight of Paris: and as for the garrison-town setting of *La Rabouilleuse*, we are told that 'Issoudun aurait engourdi Napoléon' ('Issoudun would have sent Napoleon to sleep'). Saumur, however, evokes other feelings in the young novelist. He is conscious of the melancholy charm of a stagnating community, 'Romantic' in its remoteness from the sordid money-seeking bustle of cities. The opening sentence, already mentioned, may be quoted in full to illustrate this:

Il se trouve dans certaines villes de province des maisons dont la vue inspire une mélancolie égale à celle que provoquent les cloîtres les plus sombres, les landes les plus ternes ou les ruines les plus tristes. (GF p. 27)

(In some country towns there exist houses whose appearance weighs as heavily upon the spirits as the gloomiest cloister, the most dismal ruin, or the dreariest stretch of barren land.) (P p. 33)

'Mélancolie' to the Romantic mind was a pleasurable sensation, denoting an ability to remain aloof from the superficial blandishments of society, and to remain in tune with what Wordsworth called 'old, unhappy, far-off things'. Balzac goes on to emphasize the differences between Saumur and the contemporary life of metropolitan France. He introduces local or technical terms: 'bardeaux' (laths), 'pans hourdés' (lath and plaster), 'ouvrouère' (workroom), 'merrain' (barrel-stave), 'poinçon' (a measure of 185 litres), 'copieux' (a local variant of 'copieurs'

24

– imitators). All these occur in the first paragraph, covering three pages of the French text.

Balzac seeks, then, to evoke our interest in, and sympathy with, this dull town, though he also tells us that inquisitiveness among neighbours and hostility towards strangers are rife. Yet the impression he leaves as we proceed to the next section is one of charm rather than of dullness, of wistful old-worldliness rather than of pettiness, despite the acknowledged presence of both these less delightful qualities in the town.

Gradually Balzac focuses our attention on 'la maison à M. Grandet', but first gives a description of the owner of the house. He claims that it is essential to be aware of Grandet's physical appearance, habits and history before a true appreciation of his house and family life can be formed. This idea is fundamental to Balzac's novelistic method; he was to summarize it succinctly in his evocation of the seedy boarding-house run by Mme Vauquer, which occupies the opening pages of *Le Père Goriot*: '. . . toute sa personne explique la pension, comme la pension implique sa personne' ('. . . her whole person explains the boarding-house, as the boarding-house implies her person').

In both cases, the characters (Grandet and Mme Vauquer) have a long association with their respective residences. Not only have they imposed their personalities on their houses, being in each case a rightful and despotic owner, but, in ways which they perhaps do not realize, they advertise in their very appearance the sort of home they have chosen. The unadorned, eminently practical and durable clothing worn constantly by Grandet enables us to guess that his house will display similar qualities – bare furnishings, but solid, durable and with no concessions to fashion or modernity. At the same time, it is important to recall that Balzac has devoted his first pages to an evocation of just such a house-cum-shop chosen at random along the street, and that nowhere has he hinted that life in Saumur could be otherwise than simple, bare and practical. We may note here that we never see the lifestyle of the luminaries of town society such as M. de Bonfons or Mme des Grassins. It is clear that, for Balzac, Grandet is merely the quintessential distillation of a type commonly found in this provincial backwater. He it is who represents, and carries to an abnormal level of intensity, the preoccupations of the business community of Saumur. He is *not* a freak in the community in which he lives. This is not to say that Grandet can be seen as normal in the wider context of French society, or that we are expected to approve of his conduct towards his family: but it should be apparent that the slow evocation of Saumur, and of the ways of its inhabitants, is deliberately planned so as to make Grandet a plausible figure.

To his physical description of Grandet, Balzac adds another dimension: that of history. As will be seen, Grandet's life had coincided with momentous happenings in France, and Balzac has carefully prepared his reader – his French reader, at least – for this context by subtly suggesting the history of Saumur itself. The town evokes the continuity of French society over centuries of tumult and dissension. Describing the patterns of nails on doors in the town, Balzac speaks of

des hiéroglyphes domestiques dont le sens ne se retrouvera jamais. Tantôt un protestant y a signé sa foi, tantôt un ligueur y a maudit Henri IV. Quelque bourgeois y a gravé les insignes de sa *noblesse de cloches*, la gloire de son échevinage oublié. L'histoire de France est là tout entière. (GF p. 28)

(hieroglyphs, once understood in every household, the meaning of which no one will now ever again unravel. In these symbols a Protestant declared his faith, or a Leaguer cursed Henri IV, or some civic dignitary traced the insignia of his office, celebrating the long-forgotten glory of his temporary high estate as alderman or sheriff. The history of France lies written in these houses.) (P p. 34)

This leads directly to a reference to the coats-of-arms of the nobility having been broken 'par les diverses révolutions qui depuis 1789 ont agité le pays' (GF p. 28). Thus the scene is set for the reader to appreciate the close relationship between Grandet's rise and the recent history of France. The first pages of the novel, then, convey an extraordinarily dense impression of the setting of the action in space (and in time, as we shall see), while affording a basic symbolic framework for the later action. Balzac has shown us the *narrowness* and *tortuousness* of the streets, the *obscurity* and *solidity* of the buildings, all of which prepare us for his description and analysis of Grandet himself.

The details which Balzac presents of Grandet's earlier years encapsulate the story of the French bourgeoisie since the Revolution. It was remarkably prescient of Balzac, writing in 1833, to see that the bourgeoisie would prove to be the most successful social group of the nineteenth century. True, the aristocracy had been gravely weakened by the events of the Revolution, but a restored monarchy had reinstated them and created new peers. The common people had become a force to be reckoned with in the last years of the eighteenth century, but had either returned to their earlier depressed condition or had risen to the lower ranks of the bourgeoisie. The greatest social force had been the army, in which, under Napoleon's aegis, a man could rise from the ranks to a high position by merit and bravery. Balzac was to depict all these social nuances in later novels, but the world of *Eugénie Grandet* does not encompass the events which shook France between 1789 and 1820. Only in the use made of them by Grandet himself do the upheavals and changes of national crises impinge upon the closed world of Saumur. The sale of the lands of Church and nobility, the flight of the *émigré* nobles, the switch from Republic to Empire – all find their echo in the opportunistic personal history of Félix Grandet. In him, Balzac embodies his view of the bourgeoisie as profiteers, cleverly seeking their own interest in the misfortunes and subsequent glory of their country, and ready to endorse each of the successive regimes which followed the Revolution of 1789.

So it is that Grandet, a master cooper, buys land confiscated from the Church and sold off cheap by the State. To do this he uses the dowry of the wife he has recently married (who was, we learn in due course, a member of the aristocracy and in line for several important inheritances). This purchase causes the townsfolk to dub him a revolutionary, though Balzac carefully informs us that economics, not politics, were his motive – he had decided to invest in vine-growing. During Napoleon's consulate (1799–1804) he was elected mayor, in which capacity he was able to enhance the value of his property by judicious road-building. When Napoleon became Emperor, Grandet's 'revolutionary' reputation caused him to lose office, but he obtained the Légion d'Honneur. His history since that time concerns the development of his capital, which reflects the preoccupations of the bourgeoisie under the Bourbon monarchy, restored in 1815.

Balzac hints at disapproval of Grandet's activities, but all are perfectly legal. To marry an ugly heiress at the age of forty denotes calculation rather than passion, and the description of Eugénie as 'fruit de leurs légitimes amours'* is certainly ironic. The Church lands were acquired 'légalement, sinon légitimement', and the fact that the 'excellents chemins' also 'menaient à ses propriétés' is stated blandly, without overt condemnation. During the period of revolutionary excesses, Grandet had opposed the sale of the lands of *émigré* nobles, perhaps foreseeing that their good-will would be useful later; but he sold barrels of wine to the revolutionary army, for which he received more Church lands in payment. Grandet always acts legally: he is not a trickster, and his manoeuvres to fob off his brother's creditors later in the story are legitimate if not laudable.

Balzac concludes this lengthy introduction to the action of his novel with a famous description of Grandet's appearance, and some hints as to his nature. A lengthy passage gives examples of his minute calculations. Unlike the elderly misers from whom his wife eventually inherits, Grandet does not worship money only for itself. His known wealth

* A phrase omitted in the Penguin translation – 'fruit of their lawful loves'.

27

makes him the biggest taxpayer ('le plus imposé') in the district, hence something of a local hero. Balzac notes such calculation as the blocking-up of windows in the country houses he owns so as to avoid tax on them; and the planting of poplars, which, Grandet later reveals, are by the river-side so as to be watered by the State – river-banks being common land. He knows exactly when to sell casks or wine at the best price, and keeps his vintages until they mature.

Financièrement parlant, Monsieur Grandet tenait du tigre et du boa. (GF p. 32)

(In matters of finance, Monsieur Grandet combined the characteristics of the tiger and the boa constrictor.) (P p. 40)

This amusing but chilling parallel matches Grandet's physical presence. Balzac gives us his stature ('cinq pieds') and even the circumference of his legs! He is short and stocky, as though even flesh were the object of his economies. Young men who know no better joke about his salt-and-pepper hair as being 'silver and gold'. But his staring gaze evokes the mythical basilisk whose glance turned men to stone. He has 'significant' bumps on his forehead – Balzac gave credence to Gall's theories on phrenology, the practice of character-reading by bumps on the cranium. His straight chin is matched by unbending lips, and his nose bears a wart, whose movement can be taken as an indicator of Grandet's inner excitement where money is concerned.

Details of Grandet's clothing confirm his economy. Never modifying his dress, he clings (even in 1819) to the fashions of 1791, from the leather thongs which fasten his shoes to the Quaker-style hat on which he rests his gloves, with a precise indifference to modishness. This economy in clothing extends to his household, since his wife and daughter are expected to make do with two dresses a year; among the known expenses attributed by Balzac to Grandet, only his renting of chairs in church for his womenfolk could be considered an extravagance.

An account of Grandet's reasons for cultivating the society of Cruchot and des Grassins, and of his methods of inciting them to rivalry, concludes this extensive introduction to the action; it also serves as a transition, since we feel that we are witnessing this redoubtable character in action. In fact, Balzac is recounting events leading up to the first scene of the story. This long opening section can truly be called an exposition. Like the exchanges of dialogue between characters in the opening scenes of a play, Balzac's various layers of description, exemplification and explanation constitute an initiation of the reader into a world which, even to Balzac's contemporaries, contained elements which must arouse curiosity. Moreover, as will be seen, the action has a great element of theatricality and Balzac can now proceed to show his characters in a situation which bears many points of resemblance to that of a stage play.

5 The Action of the Novel

As the summary of the plot has revealed, the action of *Eugénie Grandet* is straightforward, lacking in complexity. The two threads of plot, centring respectively on Grandet's obsession with money and Eugénie's love for Charles, are so close as to be practically one. Not only do they take place under the same roof, they also make contact at crisis points in the story, and may even be considered to be similar. In this early tale, Balzac wisely eschews the proliferation of minor characters and sub-plots typical of his longer, later novels – even of *Le Père Goriot*, his next major composition. In doing so, as has been noted, Balzac situates *Eugénie Grandet* in that stream of 'classical' French novels which explore a single situation in depth.

At the same time, the mechanics of the plot are sharply defined, each turn of the action vividly described. The precision of the action, the compactness of the setting and the boldly drawn characters give *Eugénie Grandet* the atmosphere of a theatrical work, and, indeed, the novel has been successfully adapted for both stage and television. The plot falls naturally into a sequence of 'scenes':

Scene 1. Charles arrives in Saumur during Eugénie's birthday celebration.

Scene 2. Next day, he learns of his father's suicide. Eugénie's feelings blossom into love.

Scene 3. Eugénie persuades Charles to take her 'douzain' and accepts his 'nécessaire' in trust.

Scene 4. On New Year's Day, Grandet learns of Eugénie's action and punishes her.

Scene 5. Two years later. A confrontation over the 'nécessaire'.

Scene 6. Four years later. Grandet on his deathbed.

Scene 7. In June of that year, Eugénie hears from Charles and decides to marry de Bonfons.

A certain amount of linking material would be omitted if only these scenes were to be staged – notably Grandet's consultations with his advisers, and Mme Grandet's death. Scenes which the reader may recall as having occurred only once will be seen to have formed a part of that tedium separating the crisis-points listed above: evocations of Eugénie confiding in her mother, Eugénie longing for news of Charles,

Grandet's decline towards death. Other 'episodes' are narrated as asides, weeks or months being condensed into a few lines: such are the lapse from virtue of M. des Grassins in Paris, or Cornoiller's courtship of Nanon.

A glance at the relative length of the 'scenes' listed above reveals that by far the greater part of the action is devoted to scenes 1, 2 and 3. Later stages of the plot occupy less than a fifth of the novel. Balzac's time-sequence, it has already been shown, involves him in some sleight-of-hand, but the effect of the disproportionate emphasis on events immediately following the arrival of Charles is to concentrate the reader's attention on the details of behaviour, and on the gradual awakening of Eugénie's feelings. To borrow terms from the cinema, the result is not so much slow-motion lyricism as a zooming-in to fix certain gestures, certain thoughts, certain clashes, which a more distant viewer might not have observed. It must be said that if Balzac gives such weight to these few days when Charles is with Eugénie, he arranges the more violent scenes between father and daughter as emotional counterweights: less extended, but telling. The reader may well feel that Eugénie's quarrels with her father occupy more space than is in fact the case. Thus Balzac's skill ensures that we do not perceive the work as lopsided.

This balance between the lengthy treatment of early scenes and the brevity of later confrontations highlights one of the triumphs of Balzac's art in *Eugénie Grandet*. He appreciates that, in the story he is about to tell, the action is strictly circumscribed by the nature, experience and relationship of the Grandets, and that the small-town setting and the cramping lifestyle of the family will determine the scale of the drama. The extravagant gesture, the operatic denunciation, would be unconvincing here (literally so – no operatic treatment of *Eugénie Grandet* exists, or at any rate, survives). Balzac unerringly judges the scale of Eugénie's acts of defiance. By normal criteria these are almost laughably trivial. She brings the sugar-bowl back to the table when her father has removed it; she coaxes Nanon into baking a special cake, the ingredients to be bought as extras; she obtains a fine wax candle for Charles's room, rather than the coarse tallow one which Grandet would give him. Balzac ensures, however, that the reader appreciates Eugénie's actions as truly heroic. The notion of 'heroine' in the sense of one who performs deeds of outstanding bravery surely applies to Eugénie, if the reader is prepared to make the necessary mental adjustment of scale from that normally applied. Balzac at one point does this for us, when Eugénie defies her father by replacing the sugar-bowl on the table, 'en contemplant son père d'un air calme'.

Certes, la Parisienne qui, pour faciliter la fuite de son amant, soutient de ses faibles bras l'échelle de soie, ne montre pas plus de courage que n'en déployait Eugénie en remettant le sucre sur la table. L'amant récompensera sa Parisienne qui lui fera voir orgueilleusement un beau bras meurtri dont chaque veine flétrie sera baignée de larmes, de baisers, et guérie par le plaisir; tandis que Charles ne devait jamais être dans le secret des profondes agitations qui brisaient le cœur de sa cousine, alors foudroyée par le regard du vieux tonnelier. (GF pp. 87–8)

(Certainly no Parisian lady, helping her lover to escape by holding the weight of his silk rope ladder with her weak arms, shows greater courage than Eugénie showed then, in putting the sugar back on the table. The Parisian will have her reward when she proudly displays to her lover a beautiful arm covered with bruises; each bruise will be kissed and bathed in tears, and pain forgotten in pleasure: while Charles would never have the remotest conception of the deadly terror that shook his cousin's heart, while she stood there stricken by the lightning of the old cooper's look.) (P p. 113)

The 'silken ladder' comes from the conventions of Romantic drama.* We note that Balzac uses the present tense ('soutient', 'montre') to describe the Parisian exploit, thereby implying that such escapades are possible in the Paris of the 1830s (we may think of Julien Sorel's climb to the window of Mathilde de la Mole in Stendhal's *Le Rouge et le noir* (1830), when a more prosaic wooden ladder is used). The use of so extravagant a comparison to highlight Eugénie's heroism is corrected when Balzac continues by pointing out that Eugénie's daring will receive no Romantic reward.

Such small acts of heroism as Eugénie can perform during Charles's stay with his relatives lead to the loan of her 'douzain', and this to the major confrontations with her father over that loan, and over the 'nécessaire'. Here the drama is heightened to a pitch approaching melodrama, but the reader accepts this heightening since Eugénie's earlier actions have prepared us for the climax to the growing conflict between father and daughter. This conflict must now be examined in detail.

---

* A play of that name by de Planard provided the plot of Rossini's opera *La Scala di Seta*, produced in Venice in 1812. Balzac, who loved Rossini's music, probably knew it.

6   The Conflict between Grandet and Eugénie

The novel seems to divide the reader's interest between Eugénie and her father, and sets the two characters in opposition to each other in several ways: thus they represent age versus youth, male versus female, heartlessness versus love, getting versus spending. Martin Turnell, in his consideration of *Eugénie Grandet* in *The Novel in France* (1950), maintains that all the interest of the work resides in the portrayal of Grandet and of his transactions. No doubt many modern readers would agree with this verdict, since Grandet presents by far the most striking character. Eugénie partakes, after all, of the convention of the small-town heroine familiar to us from many later novels, plays and films, the girl whose life is changed by the impact of a stranger passing through. Yet we cannot overlook the title chosen by Balzac. *Eugénie Grandet* directs the reader's attention towards his heroine. She is, we must concede, the only character who develops as a result of the action – not even Charles does this. She matures as her insights deepen, and as she undertakes acts of heroism and renunciation which Balzac clearly links to her religious beliefs. She is, indeed, as much her mother's daughter as she is her father's. In the space of six weeks (from 'au milieu du mois de novembre' to 'le premier janvier 1820') Eugénie progresses from her status as the girl who requires her father's consent before she can accept a birthday gift to that of the defiant woman whose confrontation with her father reveals an implacable logic.

– Etais-je libre, oui ou non, d'en faire ce que bon me semblait? Etait-ce à moi?
– Mais tu es un enfant.
– Majeure. (GF p. 148)

('Was I free, yes or no, to do as I pleased with it? Was it mine?'
'But you are a child!'
'I'm of age.') (P p. 194)

We see how this stage has been reached as we trace a gradual change in Eugénie's attitude towards her father. Her first timid intervention on behalf of Charles meets with a rebuff from her father.

– Mais, mon père, Monsieur a peut-être besoin de quelque chose, dit Eugénie.
– Il a une langue, répondit sévèrement le vigneron. (GF p. 53)

33

('But, father, perhaps he needs something to eat or drink after his journey,' said Eugénie.
'He has a tongue,' replied the winegrower harshly.) (P p. 68)

Shortly after this, she goes to help her mother and Nanon make up Charles's bed; Balzac informs us that her motives were not those of a dutiful daughter but of an inspectress, desirous of checking that all was up to the standard she had already set for Charles's welcome:

Eugénie se croyait déjà seule capable de comprendre les goûts et les idées de son cousin. (GF p. 58)

(Already Eugénie believed that only she held the key to her cousin's tastes and ideas.) (P pp. 74–5)

Indeed, the first sign of her new-found self-confidence is her despotic countering of all the preparations made by her seniors. We are told that Nanon's hesitations about obtaining sugar and wax candles are dispelled by 'la première plaisanterie que sa jeune maîtresse eût jamais faite' (GF p. 59).

The next day, Grandet brutally informs his family of his brother's suicide. Eugénie's tears produce an unsympathetic remark from her father.

Eugénie apprit en ce moment que la femme qui aime doit toujours dissimuler ses sentiments. Elle ne répondit pas. (GF p. 81)

(In that moment, Eugénie learned that a woman in love must always hide her feelings. She made no answer.) (P p. 105)

When, close to noon, Grandet tells Charles of his father's suicide without seeking to soften the blow, he compounds his brutality by commenting to the women:

Mais ce jeune homme n'est bon à rien, il s'occupe plus des morts que de l'argent. (GF p. 90)

('But that young man is good for nothing; his mind runs more on dead folk than it does on the money.') (P p. 116)

Balzac identifies this moment as the decisive factor which turns Eugénie away from Grandet.

Eugénie frissonna en entendant son père s'exprimant ainsi sur la plus sainte des douleurs. Dès ce moment, elle commença à juger son père. (GF p. 90)

(Eugénie shuddered to hear her father speak in this fashion about the most sacred of all sorrows. From that moment she began to criticize her father in her mind.) (P p. 116)

Later, after Grandet's departure,

Eugénie et sa mère respirèrent à leur aise. Avant cette matinée, jamais la fille n'avait senti de contrainte en présence de son père; mais depuis quelques heures, elle changeait à tous moments et de sentiments et d'idées. (GF p. 92)

(. . . Eugénie and her mother breathed more freely. The girl had never before that morning felt constraint in her father's presence; but in the last few hours her feelings and her ideas had been rapidly changing.) (P p. 119)

Thus Balzac prepares us for Eugénie's disregard of her father's certain anger as she decides to give her money to Charles. No doubt she would have fallen in love in any case; but her growing revulsion from the standards applied by Grandet is instrumental in causing her to come to that decision unaided. In turn, her love gives her the courage to sustain the violence of Grandet's wrath and the subsequent attempt to recover the gold from Charles's 'nécessaire'.

Grandet, on the other hand, undergoes no such transformation. Throughout those episodes of the novel in which he appears, his character, thoughts and reactions remain as unchanging as his dress. Balzac notes, for example, how he folds his brother's letter precisely along its original creases, a typically economical gesture, but one which also shows us that Grandet will betray no emotion at the news he has just read. Instead of change, Balzac uses gradual revelation of existing traits to maintain our interest in Grandet, whose character displays different facets according to his mood   his wife and daughter have a highly developed sensitivity to changes of humour – or indeed according to circumstance. We may, for example, be unprepared for his comic stammer, but we realize that it has a purpose in furthering the miser's ends.

Balzac mentions only two modifications to Grandet's persona as delineated in the early pages of the novel. The first is that, with age, he becomes more attached to the physical presence of gold, and less content merely to use it. The second springs from his decline into old age, and the need to initiate Eugénie into his affairs. The two combine in one of the most striking episodes in the story, as the dying man seeks to clutch the gold crucifix, and warns his daughter that accounts will be demanded of her in the hereafter.

Grandet, in fact, exemplifies one of the mainstays in Balzac's fiction, the obsessive character, victim of what his creator calls 'la monomanie'; in this case, a fixation on money and its power. The opposition between Grandet and his daughter could not, it seems, be more complete.

And yet Eugénie too is a monomaniac, and Charles becomes her object. Of Charles, Balzac writes, 'le sang des Grandet ne faillit pas à sa destinée' (GF p. 172) ('Charles was a Grandet, and the fatal weaknesses of his Grandet blood did not fail to reveal themselves' – P p. 226), and the same might be said of Eugénie. 'Elle est plus Grandet que je ne suis Grandet,' exclaims her father perceptively as she confronts him (GF p. 149) ('She's more of a Grandet than I am myself' – P p. 194), just after Balzac has indicated that Eugénie has now equalled her father in strength of character, 'devenue aussi rusée par amour que son père l'était par avarice' (GF p. 148) ('if cupidity had made Grandet wily, love had taught his daughter to be wary' – P p. 193).

How, we may ask, did Eugénie reach this new state? Here we may pause to trace the effects wrought in her by her awakening passion. One of the first signs of nascent love is an animation which the earlier scenes have shown to be lacking in her, since she seemed to be merely a pawn in a power game. Balzac demonstrates the immediate effect of this new liveliness in Eugénie when she goes to help arrange her cousin's room:

. . . elle arriva fort heureusement pour prouver à sa mère et à Nanon, qui revenaient pensant avoir tout fait, que tout était à faire. (GF p. 58)

(. . . she came very luckily, just in time. Her mother and Nanon were leaving the room, thinking that they had done everything, but she convinced them that everything was still to do.) (P p. 75)

Eugénie, in fact, takes over from her mother, the nominal mistress of the house, and from Nanon, its real mistress, and Balzac tells us why:

Eugénie se croyait déjà seule capable de comprendre les goûts et les idées de son cousin . . . Il lui avait plus surgi d'idées en un quart d'heure qu'elle n'en avait eu depuis qu'elle était au monde. (GF p. 58)

(Already Eugénie believed that only she held the key to her cousin's tastes and ideas . . . More sudden inspirations had crowded into her mind in a quarter of an hour than she had had in all the years since she was born.) (P pp. 74–5)

One delightful feature of Balzac's portrayal of this transformation in Eugénie is that he invites us to smile at her. Here, most of all, she evokes the impetuous heroines of some of Jane Austen's novels: Catherine Morland of *Northanger Abbey*, or Marianne Dashwood of *Sense and Sensibility*. Her pretensions, mentioned above, are certainly more credible than any her mother or Nanon could lay claim to, but they are none the less amusing, and Balzac's detailing of her efforts to modify the bleakness of Charles's room shows how, 'légère comme un oiseau', she wheedles and bullies the two older women, dispelling Nanon's doubts with 'la première plaisanterie que sa jeune maîtresse eût jamais faite' (GF p. 59). This humorous tone is resumed next morning as Eugénie anxiously fusses:

Elle allait, venait, trottait, sautait. Elle aurait bien voulu mettre à sac toute la maison de son père ... Après deux heures de soins, pendant lesquelles Eugénie quitta vingt fois son ouvrage pour aller voir bouillir le café, pour aller écouter le bruit que faisait son cousin en se levant, elle réussit à préparer un déjeuner très simple, peu coûteux ... (GF p. 83)

(She came and went, ran in and out from one room to another, danced here and there. She would gladly have ransacked her father's house from top to bottom ... After two hours of busy occupation, in the course of which Eugénie left her work twenty times at least to go and watch the coffee boiling, or listen for sounds from her cousin's room announcing that he was getting up, she had succeeded in preparing a very simple, very inexpensive lunch ...) (P p. 107)

Her mother recognizes this quality of amusing yet touching enthusiasm in some of her remarks: 'Tu est folle', or, as Eugénie declares that she will learn to operate the Chaptal coffee-maker vaunted by Charles, her mother's tender 'Enfant' to her speaks worlds of affection, some sadness, but surely some amusement too. Lastly may be quoted Eugénie's anxiety, during the secretive transfer of Grandet's wealth at dead of night, lest her father might be having her cousin kidnapped. We may be amused by Eugénie's melodramatic fears, but the incident also confirms that we are in the presence of an obsession. At this point, the two monomanias cross. Eugénie can now think only of Charles, and we can see that Balzac has been drawing together the two obsessions to a point where they must inevitably collide. The novelist's skill here is superb, and if he crowns it a few pages later by pointing out a thematic link, surely this can be accepted as a legitimate ploy.

Ainsi, le père et la fille avaient compté chacun leur fortune; lui, pour aller vendre son or; Eugénie, pour jeter le sien dans un océan d'affection. (GF p. 123)

(So both father and daughter had counted their wealth that night; he, for the purpose of selling his gold; Eugénie to cast it abroad upon an ocean of affection.) (P p. 160)

The element of playful, girlish animation shows, of course, only one side of Eugénie's development. Balzac frequently underlines the innocence of Eugénie's heart, culminating in the episode in which she ventures unchaperoned into Charles's room. The author comments in a way which reveals to present-day readers the unconventionality of such a scene:

Le passé d'Eugénie servira, pour les observateurs de la nature humaine, de garantie à la naïveté de son irréflexion et à la soudaineté des effusions de son âme. (GF pp. 98–9)

(. . . to observers of human nature, Eugénie's past life shows sufficient cause for her unreflecting naïveté and the impulsiveness with which she gave expression to her feelings.) (P p. 128)

In the bedroom, Charles is asleep in a chair, and fully dressed, but the boldness of such an intrusion by a young girl becomes apparent to Eugénie herself, and she flees, 'honteuse d'être venue', and Balzac draws the moral:

L'innocence ose seule de telles hardiesses. Instruite, la Vertu calcule aussi bien que le Vice. (GF p. 99)

(Only innocence dares to be so bold. Both vice and virtue (when it has acquired some knowledge) weigh their actions carefully.) (P p. 129)

Innocent, yes; but conscious, too, of an unseemly boldness, Eugénie is seen to be awakening to womanhood at the age of twenty-three. Examples of her new awareness could be multiplied, but a few will suffice. Thus, on hearing her father say that she will never be Charles's wife:

Les lointaines espérances qui pour elle commençaient à poindre dans son cœur fleurirent soudain, se réalisèrent et formèrent un faisceau de fleurs qu'elle vit coupées et gisant à terre. (GF p. 79)

(The vague hopes of happiness far in the future which had begun to grow in her heart had suddenly sprung up and burst into perfect bloom, and now her treasure of flowers was cut down before her eyes and flung on the ground.) (P p. 102)

Again, as she weeps for Charles's misfortune, Balzac notes:

La compassion, excitée par le malheur de celui qu'elle aime, s'épanche dans le corps entier d'une femme. (GF p. 81)

(Her heart ached, as a woman's heart does ache when, for the first time in her life, her whole being is filled with compassion for the sorrow of someone she loves.) (P p. 104)

Later, within the space of a few paragraphs, Balzac uses both 'femme' and 'jeune fille' to designate Eugénie, showing that she is not fully the one, but is no longer entirely the other: 'cet instinct, cette finesse de femme' guides her to distract Charles from brooding on his father's death (GF p. 93), but the all-embracing glance she throws on his belongings is 'ce regard des jeunes filles qui voient tout en un clin d'œil' (GF p. 94).

After the girlish deceptions triggered by her cousin's arrival, nothing displays Eugénie's new personality so well as the courage she shows in risking her father's wrath. The cajoling of Nanon to obtain a 'galette' is her first victory, but she quails before her father's presence, and replies 'Non, non' to Nanon's outright request for confirmation of Eugénie's wishes. Her father unexpectedly softens and grants the release of provisions. He is as yet unaware of such extravagances as extra candles and sugar, so that the real confrontation is deferred until Grandet returns home during Charles's meal. The panic reactions of the womenfolk do not prepare us for Eugénie's defiance of her father as she replaces the sugar on the table, surely one of the most critical moments of her development, and one already considered. An astonishing attempt to be kittenish with her father ('Goûte donc à ma conserve, papa!') produces only the ominous reaction, 'Oh! si on ne les arrête, elles mettront Saumur au pillage pour vous, mon neveu' (GF p. 88) ('Oh! if they aren't stopped they will loot the whole town of Saumur for you, nephew' – P p. 114).

This incident reveals two points of interest. Firstly, Eugénie's badinage conceals sadness, since she knows what grief is awaiting Charles. Thus she has learnt to hide her true feelings. Secondly, Grandet's words chillingly recall Balzac's statement earlier in the chapter, that Eugénie 'aurait bien voulu mettre à sac toute la maison de son père' (GF p. 83). The coming conflict between two obsessions is beginning to loom. It reaches the surface in a later scene as Grandet, unable to resist boasting of his financial coup in selling his gold, replies to Eugénie's apparently artless calculation of his profit, and is told by her, 'Eh, bien, mon père, vous pouvez facilement secourir Charles' (GF p. 95) ('Well, then, father, you can easily help Charles' – P p. 123). This from a girl who only days before knew nothing of money, to whom terms such as 'un million' and 'faire faillite' had to be explained, reveals a sudden awareness of the power of money. Her father's angry reaction and his threats to send her away show a realization in him of the power of love, for an element of jealousy is detectable in Grandet's reply; he is no longer the only man in his daughter's life. The confrontation culminates in a riposte which encapsulates several emotions. Having asked what Charles is doing, Grandet is told by Eugénie, 'Il pleure son père' (GF p. 95) ('He is weeping for his father' – P p. 123).

How brilliantly Eugénie's reply suggests that she has noted her father's lack of tears for his brother; how subtly Balzac suggests that the two father–child relationships are to be contrasted, and that the harsh monosyllables spat out by Eugénie mark a state of hostilities between

Grandet and his daughter. Conflict has become their mode of com-munication; a passive, dutiful daughter has become a rebellious, critical woman, who, in turn, will cultivate her 'monomanie'.

In a telling passage of authorial comment, Balzac admits that, in the eyes of some scoffers ('quelques railleurs'), Eugénie's love could be seen as a disease ('une maladie') which 'influença toute son existence'. For that very reason, he says,

la profonde passion d'Eugénie devrait . . . être analysée dans ses fibrilles les plus délicates. (GF p. 98)

(Eugénie's passion should be traced to the source from which its most delicate fibres sprang, its roots in the depths of her nature, and analysed there . . .) (P p. 128)

Though not a disease, in Balzac's view, Eugénie's love possesses her none the less. She waits almost ten years for Charles, and, on learning of his betrayal of their love, the energies she had drawn from her obsession are expended in a single gesture: her marriage to de Bonfons and the liquidation through him of Charles's debts. (In this, she contrasts, for example, with the jilted heroine of Henry James's novel *Washington Square*, for whom revenge is the motive force of life.) Thereafter her existence loses its impetus, and the last pages of the novel show her life as drained of passion and purpose.

Even before this, though, the relationship with her father had become an armed truce. With her mother's death, Eugénie assumes some of the dead woman's resigned passivity, and, in her voluntary renunciation of her inheritance, already divests herself of a part of the force which had fuelled her resolve. By training her to replace her mother – and, indeed, to be of greater importance to him than his late wife – in the running of his household and in her knowledge of his affairs, Grandet contributes to this decline in Eugénie's vital energies. The 'mariage blanc' does nothing to revive her drooping spirits, and the novel ends with praise of Eugénie's piety, charity and greatness of soul. She may well 'marche au ciel accompagnée d'un cortège de bienfaits' (GF p. 189) ('Eugénie's way to heaven is marked by a succession of deeds of kindness' – P p. 248), but the picture the reader forms is of a defeated heroine.

7 Characterization

It will have become evident in the preceding pages that Balzac's novel offers at least two characters of absorbing interest. Eugénie and her father not only provide a dramatic and fully documented conflict; each in his or her own right exemplifies the novelist's art, possibly at its finest. Balzac may often be criticized for 'telling' rather than 'showing', for overtly orientating the reader's reactions rather than allowing him to form his own judgements. In the case of Eugénie and Grandet, however, the balance between 'telling' and 'showing' is struck. A long introduction to Grandet enables us to relish his character when we see it in action, but Eugénie has already been observed at the moment of her life's great crisis long before Balzac offers a full-length portrait of her as she sits at her window.

Balzac's skill as a creator of characters can be compared with that of Dickens. The exuberance of his larger-than-life characters and the precise placing of minor figures merit the highest praise, and in one respect at least he can be preferred to Dickens: his heroes and heroines have far more true life than the vapid dummies of some of Dickens's novels. It would be fairer to compare him with Scott, who was, after all, his principal model, and here Balzac is, to modern taste, clearly superior.

Like all novelists, Balzac must have used real-life models to some extent, and much energy has been expended in research into possible originals for his characters, notably (for *Eugénie Grandet*) Grandet himself. The possible contenders are well summed up in Pierre Citron's introduction to the Garnier-Flammarion edition. Balzac himself warned his readers against such model-seeking:

La littérature se sert du procédé qu'emploie la peinture, qui, pour faire une belle figure, prend les mains de tel modèle, les pieds de tel autre, la poitrine de celui-ci, les épaules de celui-là. L'affaire du peintre est de donner la vie à ces membres choisis et de la rendre probable.

(Literature uses the technique used by painting, which, to create a beautiful form, takes the hands of this model, the feet of that, the chest of this one, the shoulders of that one. The task of the painter is to give life to these selected limbs, and to make it look likely.)

We may ask ourselves whether it is really important to know that Balzac was aware of actual miserly businessmen living in the Loire valley; surely it is far more rewarding to see *how* he is able to make credible such a monster of avarice as Grandet. Before his eyes lay the formidable precedent of Harpagon in the comedy *L'Avare*,* by Molière, of whom Balzac said: 'Molière a fait *L'Avare*, moi j'ai fait l'avarice.' This implies that Grandet surpasses Harpagon in the range and authenticity of his avarice, and, indeed, the novelistic form allows Balzac to use precisely observed details not available to the playwright. An example of this can be seen in the external description which Balzac uses to present a character. In the case of Harpagon a traditional dress exists for the character, based on that worn by Molière himself in the part, and items of it are mentioned in the text. Photographs of actors in revivals over the last few decades reveal, however, that no immutable aspect can be ascribed to Harpagon, and, of course, each actor brings his own physique to the role. Grandet, on the other hand, springs to life in every detail of his dress, each item of which speaks of durability and economy. Balzac also links the man's personal habits to his economy of energy: his speech, as we might expect, tends to be laconic, and Balzac notes among his gestures the regular placing of his gloves at the same spot on the brim of his hat, for easy retrieval. Moreover, Balzac sustains the initial impression of this tidy (and economical) gesture by referring to it several times, thus conveying the ingrained nature of the habit. Equally, Balzac does not reveal all of Grandet's characteristics or habits at once, but produces fresh evidence at intervals, so as to maintain and extend our interest in a character basically incapable of change or development. Grandet's reactions always confirm our initial impressions of him: he eats his breakfast standing up; he always orders fires to be doused in any unoccupied room; he rarely uses violent language, but his 'par la serpette de mon père', potentially a ridiculous oath, becomes menacing as a barometer of his anger.

Balzac also shows us in action certain traits which he lists in the introductory description. The stammer which is referred to there comes

---

* Molière's comedy is set in the bourgeois society of Louis XIV, and depicts a family deeply divided by the father's avarice. Harpagon wishes to marry a young woman, Mariane, who is loved by his son Cléante. His daughter Elise secretly loves and is loved by a young stranger, Valère, who has taken up a post as Harpagon's steward. Conflicts arise between father and son when Mariane is invited to the house as Harpagon's future bride and realizes Harpagon is the father of the man she loves. Comedy abounds in scenes with servants and the marriage-broker Frosine, but the situation becomes bleak as Elise is ordered to marry an elderly man, Anselme, and Cléante is given Harpagon's curse (the only thing he does give). Cléante's valet steals a strong-box, thereby driving the miser to distraction. In the resultant confusion, Anselme is revealed to be the long-lost and wealthy father of both Valère and Mariane, and gives his consent to their marriages to Elise and Cléante.

to life in the interview with Grandet's advisers: the basilisk-like stare is turned on Eugénie more than once. In moments of crisis, Grandet always acts in character. The attempt to prise gold off Charles's 'nécessaire' corresponds with his need to know the quality and value of it; his gesture to reassure his dying wife and to exorcise her malady consists of spreading gold over her counterpane. It comes as no surprise that the culminating gesture of his life should also be a valid summary of it: his attempt to grab the gilt crucifix as he lies dying.

Both Grandet and Eugénie are the objects of extended commentary by Balzac, which serves to amplify and deepen our appreciation of them. Balzac here uses a range of approaches, which may be illustrated from his first sustained portrait of Eugénie, surprisingly late in the novel (GF pp. 70–74, P pp. 91–5). The novelist meticulously catalogues the actions marking the start of Eugénie's day, noting what is different on this special day:

... elle se leva de bonne heure, fit sa prière ... lissa d'abord ses cheveux châtains ... se lavant plusieurs fois les mains dans de l'eau pure qui lui durcissait et rougissait la peau ... Elle mit des bas neufs et ses plus jolis souliers. Elle se laça droit, sans passer d'œillets. (GF p. 71)

(... she got up earlier than usual, said her prayers ... first brushed her chestnut hair ... she washed her hands over and over again in cold spring water that roughened and reddened the skin ... She put on new stockings and her prettiest shoes. She laced herself right up, careful not to leave undone a single eyelet hole.) (P pp. 91–2)

This simple enumeration allows Balzac to display a certain humorous attitude towards Eugénie which immediately adds relief to her still somewhat bland persona. The very mild poking of fun at Eugénie's naive and guileless efforts to appear to advantage immediately humanizes her and removes her from the trap of being too goody-goody. It is implied that she usually *does* skip eyelet holes in her stays, and later information that she is ' fortement constituée' reveals that she needs all the help she can get! Equally, we smile to see that her faith in a good scrub in cold water leads to a comparison of her cousin's soft white skin with her own. All this prepares the reader for the outright comedy of Eugénie's simplicity in thinking she had done all she could to make herself attractive, 'ignorant l'art de remanier dix fois une boucle de cheveux et d'en étudier l'effet' ('she knew nothing of the art that leads a woman to try placing a curl in a dozen different positions to study the effect'): she merely ('tout bonnement') folds her arms and waits.

As in the case of Grandet, Balzac presents Eugénie by means of a detailed physical description, having first of all evoked the garden as she sees it on this fateful morning. The reader who anticipates the portrait of a beauty will be surprised. Balzac seems concerned to undercut any Romantic expectations. She has the ample form of the Venus de Milo, and 'une tête énorme'. The bloom has been taken from her skin by a mild dose of smallpox, and her nose is rather large. Eugénie, then, doesn't have the insipid beauty of a Scott heroine, or the vivacity of most of Jane Austen's ladies (though she is akin to Anne Elliot in *Persuasion*, who had also lost her bloom, and she would have been at home with Fanny Price, the mousy heroine of *Mansfield Park*, who also rises to a moral challenge). However, Balzac uses these imperfections to set off Eugénie's true beauties, and his purpose in seeming to render his heroine ordinary becomes clear as the novel progresses: her moral progress is paralleled by a greater physical beauty.

A third approach to portrait-presentation lies in comparison. We have already noted that Grandet's portrait is accompanied by animal imagery. For Eugénie, the point of reference is the flower. Gazing on the dark, secluded garden, she sees the sun strike a wall covered with 'cheveux de Vénus' (maidenhair fern: in the French text, we are being prepared for the Venus de Milo comparison). Balzac makes it clear that this is symbolic, that Eugénie's life is represented by the garden, and that the sun is hope. At another level, the flowers ('fleurs pâles', 'clochettes bleues', 'herbes fanées') are the girl herself, and the conventional use of flower imagery at the close of this long description ('Cette physionomie calme . . . comme une jolie fleur éclose . . . sur la rive de la vie où fleurissent les illusions enfantines, où se cueillent les marguerites . . .') gains by the earlier implied identification.

Another, less expected, image lies in Balzac's references to Eugénie as fit material for an artist. The Venus de Milo leads him to a comparison of her 'tête énorme' with 'le front masculin mais délicat du Jupiter de Phidéas'. But more significant is Balzac's later invocation of a Raphael madonna.

Le peintre qui cherche ici-bas un type à la céleste pureté de Marie, qui demande à toute la nature féminine ces yeux modestement fiers devinés par Raphaël . . . eût trouvé tout à coup dans le visage d'Eugénie la noblesse innée qui s'ignore . . . (GF p. 73)

(A painter, searching on this earth for a type of the celestial purity of Mary, requiring that all women's eyes should possess the proud humility that Raphael's vision gave them . . . would have seen at once unconscious innate nobility of soul in Eugénie's face . . .) (P pp. 94–5)

This comparison is developed in a surprising manner later in the story when Balzac proposes further images of Mary as a touchstone for Eugénie:

Avant la venue de son cousin, Eugénie pouvait être comparée à la Vierge avant la conception; quand il fut parti elle ressemblait à la Vierge mère; elle avait conçu l'amour. (GF p. 140)

(Before her cousin's coming Eugénie might have been compared with the Virgin before the Annunciation. When he had passed from her life she seemed like the Virgin Mother. She carried love like an unborn child.) (P p. 183)

Balzac mentions Spanish art as particularly rich in representations of these two aspects of Mary. Taken with reference to Raphael, these evocations of paintings soften the feelings that some readers may have, that Balzac has here committed an error of taste almost amounting to blasphemy. The tone of the novel shows that his intentions are, on the contrary, lofty, and the image is being used to make the point that Eugénie is as pure after her encounter with Charles as she was before it. Her experience has not corrupted her.

Speech is another way of sharpening the presentation of characters. Here it is Grandet who acquires the greatest additional density through Balzac's extraordinarily varied and vivid use of numerous turns of phrase to evoke mood and circumstance. Already in his initial portrait of Grandet, the novelist has listed 'quatre phrases exactes autant que des formules algébriques' which serve him in all his business dealings: 'Je ne sais pas', 'Je ne puis pas', 'Je ne veux pas', 'Nous verrons cela' (GF p. 34). The last of these is re-used tellingly when the hypersensitive Mme Grandet recognizes in her husband's 'voix caressante' when he says 'Nous verrons cela' (GF p. 159) a sign of his change of heart towards Eugénie: equally, Eugénie's own use of the phrase after her father's death confirms that the spirit of the Grandets is still alive (GF p. 183). Grandet's range of vocalization is truly amazing. Balzac weaves together his gaiety and outbursts of song, his playful address to Eugénie, 'fifille', his cutting 'Madame Grandet' to his wife, the oath which expresses his anger, 'par la serpette de mon père', his occasional flashes of compassion for Nanon, 'Cette pauvre Nanon', and, most memorably, the pure comedy of his feigned stammer, which provides an admirable example of his power over others, leading them into statements they did not intend to make. This variety ensures a tone which is both recognizably Grandet's and yet unpredictable – the reader, like Eugénie and her mother, tries to read into Grandet's first words in each scene what his current humour may be.

One of Balzac's most telling effects concerns the use of 'tu' and 'vous'

– a device difficult to render in English. The moment of transition from the formal 'vous' to the intimate 'tu' between Charles and Eugénie comes, appropriately, as Charles speaks of marriage:

- Chère Eugénie, un cousin est mieux qu'un frère, il peut t'épouser, lui dit Charles. (GF p. 134)

('Dear Eugénie, a cousin is better than a brother, he can marry you,' said Charles.) (P p. 174)

Barely a page of text covers the days during which the lovers said 'tu' before Charles's departure, but Balzac ensures that the reader is aware of this more intimate form as Eugénie opens Charles's letter, years later:

Ma chère cousine . . .
– Je ne suis plus Eugénie, pensa-t-elle. Et son cœur se serra.
Vous . . .
– Il me disait *tu*! (GF p. 177)

(My dear Cousin . . .
'I am not "Eugénie" now,' she thought; and her heart stood still.
'You . . .'
'He never used to address me like this, like a stranger!') (P p. 232)

In each case, the English cannot convey the transition which adds so much to the emotional weight of the scene. More subtly, Balzac shows the force of Grandet's disapproval of his family's words or deeds by having him use 'vous' or 'tu'. This emerges most strikingly when Grandet learns that Eugénie no longer has her coins. 'Eugénie, qu'avez-vous fait de vos pièces?' he demands (GF p. 147), and later in the same episode he passes from one to the other. 'Je crois bien que je ne te donnerai plus rien . . . Vous méprisez donc votre père; vous n'avez donc pas confiance en lui', etc. This use of both forms in the dialogue with Eugénie extends over two pages of text, and admirably conveys the degree of rage, sternness, persuasion, contempt or scorn which Grandet is expressing at any given moment. In suggesting by this simple means a wide gamut of inflections, Balzac is reinforcing the solidity of his characterization.

Speech perhaps plays the major part in characterizing the two rival factions intriguing around Eugénie. The Cruchotins and the Grassinistes, constantly jockeying for position, reveal more than they are conscious of in their dialogues, and nowhere more plainly than when Grandet plays them off one against the other for offers of help over his brother's bankruptcy. Similarly, the skirmishes between Mme des Grassins and her opposite number, the abbé – a man in skirts – betray more than a little cattiness. The lady's mean-spirited nature shows clearly in her words to Charles, whom she has only just met, first vaunting her own position in the society of Saumur and then continuing:

> Votre oncle est un grigou qui ne pense qu'à ses provins, votre tante est une dévote qui ne sait pas coudre deux idées, et votre cousine est une petite sotte, sans education, commune, sans dot, et qui passe sa vie à racommoder des torchons. (GF pp. 59–60)

('Your uncle is a miser, and his whole mind is fixed on his vine cuttings; your aunt is a saint, and hasn't two ideas to knock against each other; and your cousin is a ninny, a common little thing with no education and no dowry, who spends all her time mending dish-cloths.') (P p. 77)

There is also that extension of speech, the letter. Four letters are written in the course of the novel; Guillaume Grandet's missive to his brother, Charles's farewell to Annette, his letter to his friend Alphonse, and the final request to Eugénie to return his 'nécessaire'. The first one provides our only contact with a man dead before the plot starts, and it comes over like an authentic voice, full of exclamation marks and rhetorical questions. Balzac has displayed great skill in all these letters, but it is the juxtaposition of Charles's pious and hypocritical 'renunciation' of Annette with the matter-of-fact practicalities of the letter to Alphonse that first alerts us to Charles's worthlessness. Perhaps the greatest triumph by Balzac in this field occurs as we reach the conclusion of Eugénie's reading of his letter to her, and, in radio terms, a 'dissolve' occurs to take us from the garden in Saumur back in time to the room in Paris where Charles's voice is heard singing a jaunty air – Figaro's 'Non più andrai' from Mozart's *Marriage of Figaro** and signing 'Votre dévoué cousin, Charles', followed by the moderately coarse oath, 'Tonnerre de Dieu! C'est y mettre des procédés' (GF p. 179). As a piece of small-scale virtuosity by the novelist, this moment represents a modest but telling success.

The novel leads any commentator to concentrate on Eugénie and her father, but in some ways Charles presents a more problematic case than either. Many readers are shocked to see him revealed as shallow and worthless, and it is tempting to see in his succession of moods a genuine development of character. Posing dandy, sincere mourner, tender lover, he seems to be progressing towards a regeneration which Eugénie's love will finally bring about, and his long (in temporal terms) absence from the action recalls the clichés of romantic fiction in which the gallant hero's absence merely emphasizes his positive qualities, to be confirmed on his return. But the reader who allows himself to be persuaded has not

---

* *Not* Almaviva's aria from that opera, as the notes to the Pléiade edition state.

read the signs. Charles's mourning may be – and probably is – sincere, but he uses it as an excuse to break with Annette. His wooing of Eugénie may not have any base aim, but he does not refuse her too-generous offer. One's doubts about the 'new' Charles ought to begin with the letter to Annette mentioned above, and continue as he insists on kissing Eugénie's bosom, into which she has just slipped his key (GF p. 134, P p. 175). Earlier, Balzac depicts Charles, not yet his cousin's suitor, literally trying to get a foot in her bedroom door (GF pp. 125–6, P pp. 163–4). Finally, we must agree with Grandet that

il n'a ni cœur ni âme, puisqu'il ose emporter le trésor d'une pauvre fille sans l'agréément de ses parents. (GF p. 151)

(He can have no heart or conscience either, to dare carry off a poor girl's money without her parents' consent.) (P p. 197)

Charles enlists our sympathy initially because of his plight as an orphan, ruined by his father's bankruptcy and cut off from his circle of friends. Most of all, we as readers are influenced by the attitudes of the Saumur household to him; the hostility of Père Grandet is almost a recommendation, and the kindliness of Mme Grandet and of Nanon reinforce approval of Eugénie's actions. However, the interest of the two older women enables Balzac to present a further aspect of Charles which we might not have anticipated: his lack of manliness. Their concern – shared by Eugénie – that Charles may find the household at Saumur too harsh may be provoked by his dandified appearance, and the reader will already have registered Balzac's amused depiction of the young man who broke his journey at Tours to have his hair recurled. Nanon, however, is the first to voice the view that Charles is 'mignon comme une femme' (GF p. 68) ('as dainty as a woman' – P p. 89), and it is she who will repeat this later, calling Charles 'quasiment joli, moutonné comme une fille' (GF p. 140) ('a lovely little gentleman, with his hair curling up over his head just like a girl's' – P p. 183). Balzac also, in his voice as novelist, directs our attention to the slightly effeminate side of Charles, which may merely be modish:

Le dandy se laissa aller sur ce fauteuil comme une jolie femme qui se pose sur un divan. (GF p. 84)

(The dandy sank gracefully into the armchair, like a pretty woman reclining on a divan.) (P p. 109)

Il est vrai que Charles, élevé par une mère gracieuse, perfectionné par une femme à la mode, avait des mouvements coquets, élégants, menus, comme le sont ceux d'une petite-maîtresse. (GF p. 85)

(It is true that Charles, who had been brought up by a gracious, charming mother, and polished by an accomplished woman of the world, was as dainty, elegant, neat in his ways as any little milliner.) (P p. 110)

Add to these hints Grandet's scornful appellation of 'mirliflor', used several times, and we begin to see another Charles, less worthy of Eugénie's love because unable to offer her the robust support she would eventually need to oppose her father, and weak enough to be led away from the vows exchanged in the garden at Saumur. Charles has already been weighed and found wanting before he temporarily disappears from the action of the novel.

8 Money

Money is one of the two poles around which the plot of *Eugénie Grandet* turns; the other, of course, is love. Balzac's world of the *Comédie humaine* is dominated by money, and this reflects its importance in Balzac's own life and in the society he depicts. Several times wealthy, several times ruined, Balzac displayed an obsession with money and yet an incapacity for handling it surprising in a novelist who, on paper, can invent the most complex financial wizardry. As for the society of the Restauration, it was to be encouraged to get rich quick by the government itself. Even before Guizot's famous 'Enrichissez-vous', the social turmoil brought about by the fall of Napoleon, the disbanding of his armies and the collapse of supportive industries meant that there were rich pickings for those willing to speculate cleverly, or able, like Grandet, to perceive certain gain before others knew of it.

Nothing is easier for the novelist than to condemn money as the root of evil, the blight of true love, the ruin of innocence. Balzac, however, holds attitudes which are far more ambivalent. Money for him is fascinating for a number of reasons. Firstly, it facilitates social contrasts, bringing together those in society who might never meet but for money (in this, Balzac's world has obvious affinities with that of Dickens). So, in *Gobseck*, the old usurer of that name meets Countess Anastasie de Restaud; so, in *La Peau de chagrin*, sudden wealth catapults Raphaël from a garret to a mansion; so, in *Le Père Goriot*, the worlds of the shabby lodging-house and of high society overlap.

Secondly, for Balzac money represents power, and that concomitant of power in Balzac's world, energy. Power is not of itself a bad thing, and ambition can only be accomplished if backed by money. Thus Grandet occupies a major place among the financiers in Balzac's novels. He is one of the few successful monomaniacs in a whole gallery of them in Balzac's fiction, since he has achieved a perfect marriage of his mania and his energies. Money, which circulates through the veins of society like blood, or which, like sperm, engenders new enterprise, has an evident symbolic value. 'Ça me réchauffe,' says Grandet of his gold, and his way of displaying affection is to display money, pouring gold over his sick wife's coverlet in order to revive her. For here is the other face of money in Balzac's world: it is the enemy of feeling, it replaces emotion, it can be given as a mere token instead of real love.

Some of this ambivalence in Balzac's attitude emerges in his treatment of Eugénie's 'douzain'. This sum, ostensibly Eugénie's dowry, is really, we are told, a form of investment for her father, since it consists of coins conserved by Eugénie and likely, as historic pieces, to increase in value. But this 'dead' money is put to use by Eugénie, becoming her most precious gift, the embodiment of her love, and no mere token as when it passed from her father's hands into hers. He still requires her to give a regular account of the coins; she will tender them without hope of or desire for any return other than Charles's affection, of which she is sure. The 'douzain' itself, enumerated by Balzac as Eugénie hands the coins over, reads like a roll-call of European history, each coin redolent of great epochs of the past, and beautiful in itself. Indeed, it is Grandet rather than Eugénie who sees the artistry of these lovely coins,

qu'il voulait revoir, afin de détailler à sa fille les vertus intrinsèques, comme la beauté du cordon, la clarté du plat, la richesse des lettres dont les vives arêtes n'étaient pas encore rayées. (GF p. 123)

(which [he] asked to see, so that he could point out their intrinsic value to his daughter, and show her the beauty of the milling, the flawless bright condition of the background, the sharp-edged unworn relief of the ornate lettering. (P p. 160)

For Eugénie, these coins have no such interest – in fact, the one she received on her birthday still lies in her purse, and she willingly parts with them in order to help Charles.

Grandet's appreciation of the coins, his 'Ça me réchauffe' on his deathbed, belie his true relationship with money. This is no mere caricature miser, gloating over his possessions. Money must work for him, as it must for Molière's Harpagon and Dickens's Scrooge, and part of its value lies in the power it confers in enabling Grandet to steal a march on others. We note, too, that he is absolutely honest according to the law. He obtained his Church lands 'légalement, sinon légitimement', and Balzac lists among his qualities 'une probité sans chaleur'. He is not, however, above breaking an agreement with his fellow traders.

On Grandet, money confers power, energy and satisfaction. His greatest coup comes with the fobbing-off of his brother's creditors, playing off Cruchotins against Grassinistes in the process. Here, as before, Balzac refers us to the scale of the novel, for, as Grandet is about to go into action to obtain his ends, the novelist reminds us that he is, after all, merely a provincial businessman:

Si le maire de Saumur eût porté son ambition plus haut, si d'heureuses circonstances, en le faisant arriver vers les sphères supérieures de la société, l'eussent envoyé dans les congrès où se traîtaient les affaires des nations, et qu'il s'y fût servi du génie dont l'avait doté son intérêt personnel, nul doute qu'il n'y eût été glorieusement utile à la France. Néanmoins, peut-être aussi serait-il également probable que, sorti de Saumur, le bonhomme n'aurait fait qu'une pauvre figure. Peut-être en est-il des esprits comme de certains animaux, qui n'engendrent plus transplantés hors des climats où ils naissent. (GF p. 105)

(If the Mayor of Saumur's ambitions had been aimed higher, if by good fortune he had risen to a higher social sphere, where he might have become a delegate to the congresses that decide international affairs, and he had there used the genius developed in him by his striving to achieve his own narrow ends, there is little doubt that he would gloriously have served the interest of France. Yet, after all, it is equally possible that away from Saumur the worthy cooper would have cut but a poor figure. It may be true that minds, like certain animals, lose their fertility when taken from their native clime.) (P p. 137)

The strategy devised by Grandet in respect of his brother's affairs does, however, succeed brilliantly – only to be negated by Eugénie after her father's death. Nevertheless, his triumph shows that the provinces can be directly pitted against Paris and, in certain domains, stand a hope of winning.

Grandet finds great pleasure and satisfaction in all his financial dealings, from the petty recouping of a part of his wife's dress allowance and the constant delays in settling with Cornoiller, to his coup in exploiting the dearth of gold at the Nantes shipyards by selling his barrelloads of coins at the best price – and by night, in secret, which adds to the pleasure of the game for him. The discomfiture of his rivals, the proof of his own superiority, increases his store of vital energy, which Balzac brilliantly equates with his habitual conservation of personal energy – witness his sparing gestures, his ritual habits.

Balzac also offers an analysis of the miser's strength:

Tout pouvoir humain est composé de patience et de temps. Les gens puissants veulent et veillent. La vie de l'avare est un constant exercice de la puissance humaine mise au service de la personnalité. Il ne s'appuie que sur deux sentiments: l'amour-propre et l'intérêt, mais l'intérêt étant en quelque sorte l'amour-propre solide et bien entendu, l'attestation continue d'une superiorité réelle, l'amour-propre et l'intérêt sont deux parties d'un même tout, l'égoïsme. (GF p. 100)

(All human power is achieved by a compound of patience and time. The people who accomplish most are the people who exert their will to watch and wait. A miser's life is a constant exercise of every human faculty in the service of his own personality. He considers only two feelings, vanity and self-interest: but as the achievement of his interest supplies to some extent a concrete and tangible tribute to his vanity, as it is a constant attestation of his real superiority, his vanity and the study of his advantage are two aspects of one passion – egotism.) (P p. 130)

Balzac's initial generalization here ('Tout pouvoir humain . . .') clearly broadens the scope of his consideration of avarice to include other obsessions, though not, it would seem, love, since this passion eschews self-interest. Once again, the opposition of Eugénie to her father in the scheme of Balzac's novel is evident.

To modern readers, the financial transactions at the heart of many of Balzac's works form an obstacle to enjoyment. Need we worry, though, about the details of these? Probably not, since the main point is clear enough: between the vast sums manipulated by Grandet and the tiny but cumulative economies practised in his family circle there is a great gulf, a contrast basic to the novel. The value of money and the relative cost of goods have changed so much since Balzac's day that calculation of equivalents is both difficult and pointless. Even in the 1830s the value of money fluctuated, as is evident from the different kinds of 'livres' referred to:

Le mot 'en livres' signifie sur le littoral de la Loire que les écus de six livres doivent être acceptés pour six francs sans déduction. (GF p. 132)

(The expression 'in livres' means among inhabitants of the Loire valley that a crown of six livres is to be accepted as worth six francs, without deduction.) (P p. 172)

This apparent clarification in fact confuses us, since the 'écu' is commonly reckoned at three francs, not six, and the reader may be surprised to see 'livre' and 'franc' equated. The franc represented a standardization imposed on all the old, variable monetary systems of pre-Revolutionary France. A decree of 1819 had fixed the 'écu de six livres' at five francs eighty – hence Grandet's precise use of 'francs sans déduction', i.e. Charles will not lose twenty centimes per livre in selling his jewellery. Balzac persists in using such older terms as 'livre', 'écu' and 'louis', partly because they were familiar to his readers, but also to show the provincial nature of Grandet's transactions. The 'louis' was of variable value, most often ten francs, while a 'napoléon' stood at twenty francs, or, if 'double', at forty.

The value of gold was evidently variable, as Grandet's haste to reach Nantes before possible competitors shows. He sold for 14,000 francs, which he took in

. . . des bons royaux qui lui portaient intérêt jusqu'au jour où il aurait à payer ses rentes. (GF p. 127)

(. . . a government certificate . . . which would bear interest until the day when the money was transferred into the funds.) (P p. 165)

This eventually brings in 600,000 francs in interest.

The details of the settlement of Guillaume Grandet's estate can be briefly summarized. They fall into three parts:

1. Des Grassins, acting for Grandet of Saumur, sells up all the dead man's effects, and uses the money to pay 47 per cent of the sum owed to each creditor. They are lulled into thinking all will be well, and do not press. The final debt is 1,200,000 francs. Grandet declares he cannot act without Charles's consent.

2. Years later, Charles returns to France and informs des Grassins that he has no intention of paying his father's debts. Des Grassins intends finally to declare the estate bankrupt, which had not been done until Charles could be informed.

3. Eugénie steps in with 1,500,000 francs to pay off all outstanding debts with interest. As her future husband de Bonfons has pleasure in informing Charles, Eugénie's private fortune has dipped from nineteen to seventeen millions by this act of generosity.

In any case, she and her husband will have a joint *income* of 750,000 francs (or 'livres', to quote de Bonfons!) per year from their investments. Charles claims in his letter to Eugénie to have an income of 80,000 francs, and proposes to marry the impoverished Mlle d'Aubrion, whose family have only 20,000 francs a year, for the sake of her title and her father's influence. As a measure of the road he has travelled, we may note that Charles values Eugénie's 'douzain' at 6,000 francs (GF p. 173), though he sends her a banker's draft for 8,000 with his letter (GF p. 179). Equally, the vast extent of Eugénie's wealth underlines the grip her upbringing exerts on her, since she continues her father's parsimonious habits.

More interesting, perhaps, than the sums involved is Balzac's use of both money and its equivalent in objects as expressions of affection. There are several other examples of this in the novel besides the obvious 'douzain'. First among them is the workbox presented by Alphonse des Grassins to Eugénie on her birthday. Flashy but cheap, this is described by Balzac as 'véritable marchandise de pacotille' (GF p. 49), significantly, in view of the importance which a real 'pacotille' or pedlar's pack will shortly assume in setting Charles on his feet. Eugénie, unused to such gifts (Alphonse's rival has brought only flowers), is delighted, but the object is close enough in function and appearance ('vermeil', or silver-gilt) to Charles's 'nécessaire' to stand revealed in retrospect as shoddy. The 'nécessaire' itself is entrusted to Eugénie as a relic of Charles's mother, but there is also a suspicion that it is in pawn with her in return for her 'douzain'. More freely distributed by Charles from his handful of trinkets are two buttons for Eugénie to make a fashionable wristlet, and a golden thimble for Mme Grandet 'qui depuis dix ans en désirait un' (in a house full of gold!). Perhaps this episode shows Charles in his best and simplest light, as it also shows Grandet to be honest in his dealings with Charles.

The 'nécessaire' again provides a symbol of values when Grandet attempts to wrest it from Eugénie. Balzac notes a change in his relationship to gold at this period: 'la vue de l'or, la possession de l'or était devenue sa monomanie' (GF p. 159) ('the sight of gold, the possession of gold . . . had become a monomania' – P p. 208). He flings himself upon the 'nécessaire' 'comme un tigre fond sur un enfant endormi' (GF p. 160), weighing it and seeking to prise off the gold. Eugénie's riposte of threatened suicide evidently equates the sacred trust of the 'nécessaire' with a human life: not for nothing is this travelling-case called a 'nécessaire', since it has become for Eugénie a source of life itself.

The last manifestation of the 'nécessaire' comes with Charles's request for it to be returned to him by the public parcels service – 'une chose pour laquelle j'aurais donné mille fois ma vie', Eugénie reminds us.

For Balzac, money represents much that he mistrusts in the new society of the Restauration. Its power to invigorate is equalled by the power of manipulation it confers upon those who possess it – Eugénie not excepted. The most striking aspect of Balzac's use of his theme of money in *Eugénie Grandet* lies in his depiction of a capitalist world, discerned and analysed before Marx wrote *Das Kapital*. Grandet stands as the quintessential capitalist in his reduction of all values to monetary ones, but around him Balzac places a number of minor examples of that persuasion: Charles, his father, des Grassins, de Bonfons, Cornoiller. Only the women could be said to assert an opposing philosophy, and that, of course, is the second pole of the novel: love.

9 Love

Eugénie Grandet is a love-story: an obvious enough statement, but one which needs to be reasserted, since so much of the novel deals with money. But Eugénie rather than her father occupies the central position, and it is her love for Charles that confers this right upon her. Uniquely among the women of the novel, she gives her love without thought of a financial connection, since Charles has few prospects after his father's death. In all other cases, money contaminates relationships, and, indeed, love seems to be absent from marriage. 'Je sais ce qui vous plaît en moi,' says Eugénie to M. de Bonfons as she informs him of her decision to marry him, thus hammering home the point already made at least three times by Balzac. The novelist has introduced a marriage for the ugly but now well-off Nanon, whom none would employ during her youth. Cornoiller's proposal follows hard on the heels of Eugénie's granting of an annuity to the faithful old servant, so that 'en moins d'un mois, elle passa de l'état de fille à celui de femme' (GF p. 168) ('In less than a month she had changed her state of life and condition from that of spinster to that of wife' – P p. 220). Though, in fact, Nanon derives prestige and support from this marriage, her age* and lack of attraction turn aside any suggestion of passion or sexual fulfilment, despite the speculation of locals that she might still be capable of bearing a child. We may also ask what love existed between M. Félix Grandet and Mlle de la Gaudinière, known to us as Mme Grandet. Balzac makes it clear that the bride was rich and well-connected, the daughter of a wealthy timber-merchant (GF p. 30, P p. 37) and in line for several legacies which duly fall into her lap all in the course of one year (1806). But she was also ugly, and her husband was twenty years older. Nothing suggests a love-match, so that Balzac's irony can surely be detected when he speaks of Eugénie as 'fruit de leurs légitimes amours'. There is a parallel here with Nanon, and an anticipation of Charles's calculated match with the unprepossessing Mlle d'Aubrion.

Thus Eugénie finds herself at the centre of a loveless family and the prize of a loveless marriage – for, in an aside never clarified, her father intimates that he has plans to marry her elsewhere than among the suitors who frequent his house:

* Balzac attributes sixty years to her as the novel opens, but only fifty-nine at the time of her marriage some years later.

Le vieux tonnelier ... se disait intérieurement: 'ils sont là pour mes écus. Ils viennent s'ennuyer ici pour ma fille. Hé! Ma fille ne sera ni pour les uns ni pour les autres, et tous ces gens-là me servent de harpons pour pêcher.' (GF p. 51)

(The old cooper ... said to himself ... 'They are all after my crowns. They have come here to spend a boring evening in hopes of winning my daughter. Ha! My daughter isn't for any of them, and these people are nothing but harpoons for my fishing!') (P p. 65)

As the novel closes, Eugénie, widowed after an unconsummated marriage, is again the object of an intrigue, this time to marry her to the elderly Marquis de Froidfond.

Thus it is apparent that by loving Charles, and by – initially at least – inspiring love in him, Eugénie is breaking a pattern. She asserts the value of the individual's feelings in a society ruled by interest. The pursuit of this love over the years sustains her; its betrayal hardens her. She represents in the novel the Romantic values of the early nineteenth century, without, apparently, having learnt them from fictional models (compare here some of the heroines of Jane Austen or Dickens).

For Eugénie has no need of such stimuli, since her life is, paradoxically, full of love even before she meets Charles. There is, first of all, her love for her parents. Balzac's depiction of the relationship between Eugénie and Mme Grandet is surely one of the triumphs of the novel, and a refutation of the charge sometimes levelled that he found the portrayal of goodness an impossible task. Throughout her life in the novel, Mme Grandet inspires in Eugénie tender and unselfish feelings which are merely intensified by her own experience of love. Behind her unprepossessing exterior, and despite her fear of her husband – 'servitude conjugale' (GF p. 44) describes her condition, and 'pauvre ilote' (GF p. 88) her status – Mme Grandet possesses a soul sensitive to her daughter's feelings. Balzac suggests that their intimacy, built up over fifteen years of shared communion at their work by the window, equals that of the 'célèbres sœurs hongroises' (GF p. 81), Siamese twins of the eighteenth century. She guesses Eugénie's emotions at a glance, and, most importantly, puts her small influence at the service of Eugénie and Charles. Arguably, she dies because of her devotion to her daughter. Balzac attributes her last illness to a tiny 'fait domestique, minime en apparence' (GF p. 142), another reminder of the small scale of the drama being played out. Because of her preoccupation with Eugénie, Mme Grandet is unable to finish knitting her woollen sleeves for the winter and hence succumbs to the chill which carries her off.

Eugénie's love for her mother deepens, from her cry of 'Oh, ma bonne

57

mère . . . je ne t'ai pas assez aimée' (GF p. 83) ('Oh! my darling mother . . . I have never loved you half enough!' – P p. 108) to the 'plus tendres soins prodigués par Eugénie' at her deathbed. Her dying words to Eugénie are recalled by her daughter at the time of her own sorrow:

> Mon enfant, lui dit-elle avant d'expirer, il n'y a de bonheur que dans le ciel, tu le sauras un jour. (GF p. 163)

('My child,' she said before she died, 'there is happiness only in heaven. You will know that one day.') (P p. 213)

> Ma mère avait raison, dit-elle en pleurant. Souffrir et mourir. (GF p. 180)

('My mother was right,' she said weeping. 'One can only suffer and die.') (P p. 236)

No such intimacy unites Eugénie with her father. However, the novelist's purpose being to show Eugénie's gradual revolt against her father's authority, the early episodes of the story depict a relationship which includes love, as well as respect and awe on Eugénie's side. Balzac tellingly introduces his heroine's name for the first time in a sentence which links her in her father's affections with her role as the future sole legatee of his fortune: 'le seul être qui lui fût réellement de quelque chose, sa fille Eugénie, sa seule heritière' (GF p. 35) ('the only being in the world who meant anything to him, his daughter and sole heiress, Eugénie' – P p. 44).

Despite the loss of her confidence in her father, despite her punishment by him, Eugénie defends his actions before his detractors (GF pp. 155–6, P pp. 203–4). She receives from her father only one spontaneous demonstration of affection, when she has agreed to renounce her claim to her mother's estate: 'Il l'embrassa avec effusion, la serra dans ses bras à l'étouffer' (GF p. 164) ('He kissed her effusively, holding her so tightly that he nearly suffocated her') – P p. 215).

The fourth member of the household, Nanon, also surrounds Eugénie with her love. Indeed, Nanon is depicted as completely devoted to others, accepting for herself a miserly share of earthly pleasures. Balzac suggests that her rejection by other employers, reluctant to engage so ugly a servant, sparked off an unconditional love for her eventual employer, Grandet, as being the man who saved her from destitution. She is particularly loyal to Grandet, though events try her fidelity sorely and oblige her to disobey her master in favour of her young mistress. Her loyalty to Grandet never wavers in public: 'la servante le défendait par orgueil pour la maison' (GF p. 155). Significantly at this later stage of the novel, Nanon's loyalties lie with the family rather than with her master.

Her grudging acceptance of Eugénie's requests for luxuries for her cousin's room and for his meals gives place to a spontaneous show of solidarity with the other women of the household, in the form of disobedience of Grandet's orders to her to deprive Eugénie of food and liberty. She becomes Eugénie's support and comfort after Mme Grandet's death, her companion in solitude and her trusted confidante. Nanon envelops the whole family in her love, and is the only character in the novel who knows a form of happiness springing from money and from marriage, if not love. As Mme Cornoiller, Nanon contrives to make of her marriage something far more positive than the 'union' of Eugénie and de Bonfons.

Undoubtedly, however, Balzac wishes to focus our attention on the love of Eugénie for Charles, and, in so far as it is real for a time, on Charles's love for Eugénie.

It must be re-stated that Balzac does not idealize his heroine. She is twenty-two or twenty-three (both ages are given) and is really 'on the shelf' by the standards of the day – Charles's choice, Mlle d'Aubrion, must be far younger, since her *mother* is only thirty-eight! Moreover, Eugénie is past thirty at the novel's close, and Balzac's own *La Femme de trente ans* informs us that thirty marks the limit of a woman's attractiveness – beyond that age, she is too old for love. The fact that Eugénie is still unattached at twenty-three indicates her importance as a pawn in Grandet's manipulation of the rival clans, who will outbid each other in their eagerness to score points in their favour as the future alliance. Eugénie is, in fact, older than Charles, but has been kept young and naive by her upbringing – unlike Charles, who already has a liaison with a married woman. Thus, Eugénie asks permission before accepting Alphonse's birthday gift, and, later, has to have the term 'un million' explained to her. To this innocent and unformed heart, the spectacle of Charles in all his tailored and pomaded glory acts as a detonator. An explosion of love commences, which Balzac analyses as it proceeds.

Balzac undoubtedly knew Stendhal's treatise on love, *De l'amour*, published in 1823. In this work, Stendhal examines the different forms of love, discerning four categories: 'amour-passion', 'amour-goût', 'amour-physique' and 'amour de vanité'. Eugénie's love for Charles belongs to the category of 'amour-passion', and to some degree Balzac follows Stendhal's analysis of the progression of such a love: admiration, fantasy, hope, the birth of love, and the famous 'cristallisation', whereby the beloved is found by the lover to be the focus of all his activities, even those apparently divorced from his love. In Eugénie's case, the growth of love is so rapid as to preclude the existence of some of these stages, though we can clearly see *admiration* in her first sight of Charles, and *hope* in her reaction to his letter of rupture to Annette. Balzac adds other elements to reinforce Eugénie's budding love for Charles. She feels *compassion* for his sorrows, *Christian charity* for his lack of resources, *family feeling* for a hitherto unknown relation, and *self-esteem* in her desire that the Grandet household should not appear too parsimonious. All these can be used by Eugénie to mask the true feelings of love to which they contribute.

The awakening of love may be fixed at the physical awakening of Eugénie on the morning following Charles's arrival. She had gone to bed with the thought, 'Sainte Vierge! Qu'il est gentil, mon cousin', interrupting her prayers; she wakes up with the doubt, 'Je ne suis pas assez belle pour lui.' It is, significantly, between these two moments that Balzac situates the long-delayed full-length portrait of his heroine as she sits at her window after making herself as pretty as she knows how. This passage has already been discussed, and some of Balzac's ploys in the presentation of Eugénie have been noted. Are we to smile at her ignorance of the arts of the Parisienne in love, who would spend an hour studying the fall of a lock of hair? We may do so, but later – much later – in the novel, we remember this innocent, naive approach to self-adornment as we read of the arts used by the ugly Mlle d'Aubrion and her mother to hook a man:

. . . la marquise d'Aubrion avait donné à sa fille un air très distingué, l'avait soumise à une hygiène qui maintenait provisoirement le nez à un ton de chair raisonnable, lui avait appris l'art de se mettre avec goût, l'avait dotée de jolies manières, lui avait enseigné ces regards mélancoliques qui intéressent un homme et lui font croire qu'il va rencontrer l'ange si vainement cherché; elle lui avait montré la manœuvre du pied, pour l'avancer à propos et en faire admirer la petitesse, au moment où le nez avait l'impertinence de rougir; enfin, elle avait tiré de sa fille un parti très satisfaisant. Au moyen de manches larges, de robes bouffantes et soigneusement garnies, d'un corset à haute pression, elle avait obtenu des produits féminins si curieux que, pour l'instruction des mères, elle aurait dû les déposer dans un musée. (GF p. 174)

(She had inherited her mother's very distinguished bearing to begin with. Then she had undergone a regimen that kept her nose for the time being reasonably flesh-coloured, had learned how to dress, acquired charming manners and the pensive expression that catches a man's attention, and makes him think that he has at last met the angel he has sought so long in vain. She had been instructed in foot tactics – had learned how to make her foot peep out and let its smallness be admired if her nose had the impertinence to turn red. Indeed Madame d'Aubrion had made the very best of her daughter. By means of wide sleeves, deceptive bodices, full flowing dresses with trimming carefully applied, and a high-pressure corset, she had produced very curious results, a feminine figure that she should have displayed in a museum for the edification and instruction of mothers.) (P pp. 228–9)

This satirical portrait, however, is still in the future of the novel, and Eugénie's present plaint, 'Je ne suis pas assez belle pour lui', reminds us that Balzac's presentation of her charms is all the more convincing for being realistic rather than romanticized. Eugénie's beauty is partly spiritual, and she will become more beautiful through the power of love. Balzac compares her, both directly and indirectly, with Parisian beauties – with Annette, for example, who never appears in the novel, but who may stand as an example of the society lady. She has been to Charles 'la plus aimable des femmes, pour lui du moins', his mistress in other words; as Charles arrives in Saumur, Annette

voyageait maritalement, ennuyeusement, en Écosse, victime de quelques soupçons auxquels besoin était de sacrifier momentanément son bonheur ... (GF p. 55)

(was making a tiresome boring journey in Scotland at the moment, in her husband's company, a victim of suspicions which demanded the sacrifice for the time being of her happiness ...) (P p. 70)

The equation of 'maritalement' with 'ennuyeusement', and of both with 'victime' and 'sacrifier', reinforces the picture of married life as a mere fiction, but also contrasts with the freshness of Eugénie's nascent emotions. When, for a moment, Eugénie's path crosses that of Annette (or Anna, to use her real name) in the episode of Charles's letter, the moral dilemma she experiences in deciding whether or not to read it marks a stage in the growth of her love:

– Je sais que je fais peut-être mal, mais je lirai la lettre, dit-elle. Eugénie détourna la tête, car sa noble probité gronda. Pour la première fois de sa vie le bien et le mal étaient en présence dans son cœur. Jusque là elle n'avait eu à rougir d'aucune action. La passion, la curiosité l'emportèrent. A chaque phrase, son cœur se gonfla davantage et l'ardeur piquante qui anima sa vie pendant cette lecture lui rendit encore plus friands les plaisirs du premier amour. (GF p. 117)

('... I know that I am perhaps doing wrong, but I will read the letter,' she said. Eugénie turned her head aside, for her high sense of honour reproached her. For the first time in her life good and evil confronted each other in her heart. Until that moment she had never had reason to blush for any action she had done. Passion and curiosity won the day. As she read, her heart beat more heavily with every phrase, and the painfully quickened sense of life that filled her drew her still more irresistibly along the path of first love's keen emotions.) (P p. 152)

Charles's letter presents another view of love relationships, as he analyses his situation, counsels Annette to accept that their affaire has no future, and announces his intention to marry, with Eugénie as his projected bride – or so it seems, since the letter remains unfinished, breaking off at this point.

Balzac devotes a long paragraph to comments on the letter and on Eugénie's naive interpretation of it. The reader is left in no doubt of Charles's 'froideur', and we learn that already he is 'habitué par les mœurs de Paris, par Annette elle-même, à tout calculer, déjà vieillard sous le masque du jeune homme' (GF p. 119). At twenty-two he has been, on the evidence of his letter, Annette's lover for four years. How can Eugénie hope to interpret the artifice of such a letter?

Balzac mentions Annette once again, when Charles consults her about his plan to marry Mlle d'Aubrion and receives her encouragement, 'enchantée de faire épouser une demoiselle laide et ennuyeuse à Charles, que le séjour des Indes avait rendu très séduisant' (GF p. 175) ('delighted to marry Charles off to such a plain and uninteresting girl. During his stay in the Indies, he had grown much more attractive' – P p. 230).

If we add to this the suggestion that his future mother-in-law was also Charles's lover, we see the cynicism with which Charles approaches marriage, despite his early leanings towards Eugénie:

Plusieurs personnes prétendent même que, pendant la traversée, la belle Mme d'Aubrion ne négligea aucun moyen de capturer un gendre si riche. (GF p. 174)

(People say that during the voyage the beautiful Madame d'Aubrion neglected no means of capturing a son-in-law so rich.) (P p. 229)

During his travels, the innocent memories of the idyll with Eugénie have been effaced from Charles's mind by a succession of 'orgies de toutes les couleurs' – literally, since his conquests have included 'les négresses, les mulâtresses, les blanches, les Javanaises et les almées' (GF p. 173).

Eugénie, unlike Charles, remains uncorrupted through years of waiting, sustained by her love. This same love, however, is the means by which she reaches maturity and attains to great moral stature. Because of love she commits acts of heroism, she learns to decide her own actions, and she comes to recognize and to value the support of her mother and Nanon. At the same time, the arrested state of her love, forced to draw sustenance from memory and deprived of a resolution in marriage, limits the transformation of Eugénie, who remains fixed in her father's sphere of influence until, and indeed even after, his death. The final blow to Eugénie's hopes, the heedless rejection by Charles of his former engagement, arrests the progress she has made towards a full realization of her potential. Her calculated marriage echoes other similar contracts in the novel, and the condition she imposes of a 'mariage blanc' ensures that her love for Charles will remain unconsummated, even with another man. Balzac's earlier comparison of Eugénie with the Virgin now assumes an ironic meaning. If her love for Charles had caused Eugénie to quicken with life like the Virgin after the Annunciation, that life is still-born, and Eugénie will remain all her life a literal virgin, never knowing motherhood or a happy marriage. Love can find an outlet only in works of charity, which may beautify the soul but cannot satisfy the body. Even the comforts bought by wealth are denied her by the imprinting of her father's habits of frugality; but in Eugénie's recourse to religion we see that her mother's message of the consolation of the spiritual life has proved equally strong.

What, then, of the idyll itself? Balzac exerts all his skill as a novelist to persuade us that the few days of Charles's stay in Saumur are crucial to Eugénie's fate. To do this, he must also convince us that Charles is sincere in his protestations, and that the baser elements in his character are susceptible to change; that he will become, in fact, that idealized Charles spoken of in his father's letter as 'probe et courageux'.

Balzac's first portrait of Eugénie shows her gazing out at the inner garden of her father's house, the very place which will be the scene of future tête-à-têtes with her cousin. The dank and unlovely scene becomes transformed for Eugénie by her newly awakened emotions:

Eugénie trouva des charmes tout nouveaux dans l'aspect de ces choses, auparavant si ordinaires pour elle . . . ces réflexions s'accordaient avec les détails de ce singulier paysage, et les harmonies de son cœur firent alliance avec les harmonies de la nature. (GF p. 72)

(Eugénie discovered a completely new charm in the scene before her, which on every previous day had seemed so ordinary and familiar . . . All the objects that her eyes rested on in this curious old garden that was her world seemed to share her feelings and her thoughts, and she herself was one with her surroundings.*) (P p. 93)

Balzac develops this theme of the pathetic fallacy, whereby Eugénie's state of mind finds its counterpart in the old garden: the sun touches a curtain of maidenhair fern, and a heavenly ray of hope shines in the heroine's heart; the sound made by a falling leaf gives a reply to the secret questionings of her soul. This literary device, well worn today, was fresher in Balzac's time, having been rediscovered by the Romantics (though the parallel between the garden and the soul goes back at least to the Middle Ages).

* The Penguin edition gives a very free translation of this passage.

For Charles, too, the garden acquires a significance, since he is pacing it with his uncle when he learns of his father's suicide:

Dans les grandes circonstances de la vie, notre âme s'attache fortement aux lieux où les plaisirs et les chagrins fondent sur nous. Aussi Charles examinait-il avec une attention particulière les buis de ce petit jardin, les feuilles pâles qui tombaient, les dégradations des murs, les bizarreries des arbres fruitiers, détails pittoresques qui devaient rester gravés dans son souvenir, éternellement mêlés à cette heure suprême, par une mnémotechnie particulière aux passions. (GF p. 89)

(In the crises of life, when we are overwhelmed by joy or sorrow, we see our surroundings with sharpened senses, and they remain for ever afterwards indelibly part of our experience. Charles scrutinized with strained intentness the box borders of the little garden, the faded autumn leaves floating to the ground, the crumbling walls, the grotesquely twisted branches of the apple trees, picturesque details which were to remain in his memory for ever, eternally bound up with the memory of that supreme hour of early sorrow, by a trick of memory peculiar to deep feeling.) (P p. 115)

Here, the novelist's perception appears strikingly acute, and indeed, years later, it is the memory of the garden that Charles evokes in his letter to Eugénie. This charging of a particular spot with strong emotional associations naturally sends the reader back to the original description, only to find that the novelist seems to be deliberately stressing the unprepossessing appearance of the garden. There seems nothing exceptional about it. Much of what it contains is utilitarian – a woodshed, apple trees, raspberry canes. But Balzac specifically characterizes its appearance as 'pas dépourvues des mystérieuses beautés particulières aux endroits solitaires ou à la nature inculte' (GF p. 71) ('not without the strange beauty of solitary spots and places left to grow wild' – P p. 92).

Such Romantic reaction to a neglected provincial garden might seem excessive if Balzac did not also, more subtly, suggest that the garden mirrors the novel in other ways. Thus much of the vegetation produces an enclosing effect: the straggling vines, the climbing plants and the bending branches of apple and walnut trees. The well may be seen as an image of Eugénie herself, pure but stagnant, and surrounded by dried-out vine shoots which imply withered hopes. Three parallel gravel paths, separated by box borders, suggest the three chief characters of the novel advancing along parallel roads in life – all are Grandets – but fated never really to meet.

This spot, then, becomes the décor of the brief idyll between Eugénie and Charles, and Balzac feels no need to retrace its contours. What seems to interest him far more is the influence of the garden, and of his feelings for Eugénie, on Charles. The novelist prefaces his account of the idyll with a series of rhetorical questions (GF p. 129, P pp. 168–9), likening the birth of love to the birth of a child, and concluding with a comment on the role of mourning in furthering this love:

... ce fut la passion première avec tous ses enfantillages, d'autant plus caressants pour leurs cœurs qu'ils étaient enveloppés de mélancolie. En se débattant à sa naissance sous les crêpes du deuil, cet amour n'en était d'ailleurs que mieux en harmonie avec la simplicité provinciale de cette maison en ruines. (GF pp. 129 30)

(... theirs was a first passion with all its childish ways, all the more tender and dear to their hearts because their hearts were surrounded by shadows. The mourning crêpe in which their love had been wrapped at its birth only brought it into closer harmony with their surroundings in the tumbledown old country house.) (P p. 169)

Balzac stresses that Charles discovers a different love from that of his stormy affair with Annette; while for Eugénie the act of deceiving her father gives to these meetings the thrill ('vivacité') of forbidden pleasures. Balzac evokes, by way of Charles's literary reminiscences, those pictures of humble contentment which form part of the German stream of Romanticism, with a specific allusion to Goethe and his creation Gretchen ('Marguerite') in Faust – but without her sexuality.

The reader, then, is led to believe that a change has been effected in Charles. His grief at his father's death, perhaps the best part of him, seems to be instrumental in leading him away from the hard, vain and indolent persona he had displayed on his arrival in Saumur. To this end, Balzac's evocation of the garden and the idyll which he locates there contribute immensely. The reader is prepared to subscribe to the Romantic view that human nature can be changed, that love will conquer. Balzac's true intentions are unobtrusively unveiled at the moment of parting:

Aucune promesse faite sur cette terre ne fut plus pure: la candeur d'Eugénie avait momentanément sanctifié l'amour de Charles. (GF p. 135)

(No more sacred promise was ever made on earth: Eugenie's transparent sincerity had momentarily sanctified Charles's love.) (P pp. 175–6)

– where 'momentanément' anticipates the betrayal to come.

The idyll itself, then, occupies far less space than the description, earlier in the tale, of the garden which sheltered it, but such is the intensity of Eugénie's love that it remains her motive force for years to come. Charles becomes her 'monomanie', and, like the gravel paths in that garden, Eugénie's life resembles her father's even more closely, yet remains separate and confined.

10   The Portrayal of a Society

The provincial way of life occupies the foreground of *Eugénie Grandet*, and one could easily take Balzac's handling of it to be a critique of a backward, blinkered and anachronistic society. As has been shown, the opening of the novel is at pains to establish the historicity of Saumur and the particular qualities of the region. The last paragraphs reveal that the action continues into Balzac's present: Eugénie still lives in Saumur and nothing in the town has really changed – the drama is personal, not communal. The matchmaking continues, and in Eugénie's household old habits go unchanged.

It would, however, be wrong to see in Balzac's presentation of a provincial society nothing but hostility. This would be to discount the affectionate tone of the novel's opening paragraphs, and the existence in the Romantic imagination of a respect for humble and outmoded things, which equates them with an idealized peasant virtue. Equally, the novel offers a number of confrontations between the provinces and Paris, which are not all to the capital's advantage. Thus, Balzac presents a corrective to the reader's expectation of a pillorying of provincial society.

The first and most striking clash between Paris and the provinces occurs when Charles arrives unannounced in his uncle's salon. Even his knock is different ('Ce n'est pas un homme de Saumur qui frappe ainsi'), and Balzac provides comparison with a snail invading a beehive or, more conventionally, a peacock being introduced into a farmyard. Later in the episode, Charles is said to have aroused the curiosity which a giraffe would have produced, the giraffe being a recent arrival at the zoo in Paris (1827). Balzac invites the reader to compare the young dandy with the standards of elegance prevalent among Grandet's guests. Although the latter include two youngish men, and would claim to be the elite of the town, they are immediately revealed to be dingy; sloppily dressed, behind the times and none too fastidious in their personal habits. Even their faces appear 'flétries ... plissées ... usées, racornies', like their garments. By prefacing this unprepossessing evocation with 'si *vous voulez* bien comprendre la surprise ...' (GF p. 56), Balzac implies a metropolitan point of view which will naturally judge the provinces to be uncouth.

Yet this criticism *follows* the long description of Charles, in which the author displays an equally detached view of the intruder. Balzac is surely inviting the reader to judge Charles a fop, in his anticipation of a splendid 'vie de château' at his uncle's home:

... il avait fait la toilette de voyage la plus coquette, la plus simplement recherchée, la plus adorable, pour employer le mot qui dans ce temps résumait les perfections spéciales d'une chose ou d'un homme. A Tours, un coiffeur venait de lui refriser ses beaux cheveux châtains; il avait changé de linge, et mit une cravate de satin noir combinée avec un col rond, de manière à encadrer agréablement sa blanche et rieuse figure. (GF p. 55)

(... Charles had put on his choicest travelling outfit, the smartest one he had which had the elegance of simplicity, the most *adorable*, to use the current epithet for perfection in man or thing. At Tours a hairdresser had been summoned to recurl his beautiful chestnut hair, and he had changed his linen and put on a black satin cravat and a round collar which framed his pale mocking face becomingly.) (P p. 71)

The deflation of Charles's anticipated social triumph is surely comic, and so is the list of his clothes for a stay in the country, all of which merit the adjective 'joli'. He has every item of equipment, 'tous les instruments aratoires dont se sert un jeune homme oisif pour labourer la vie' (GF p. 55), from horse-whip to duelling pistols. Charles entertains a particular hope of appearing 'avec la supériorité d'un jeune homme à la mode', who will confound his provincial hosts. His discomfiture on realizing that his uncle's family have no interest in Parisian life is deflating, so that Charles, as much as the provincials, is the object of Balzac's criticism. As has been pointed out, the peripheral figures of Annette and the d'Aubrions further suggest that Parisian values are meretricious. The only true emotions to emanate from Paris come in Guillaume Grandet's letter of farewell to his brother.

Nor is Paris presented as a repository of business acumen and intelligence. The creditors of Charles's estate fall victims to Grandet's wiles and are eventually recompensed through his daughter's probity. None seems a match for the financial genius of remote Saumur. Balzac implies, however, that Grandet might not have excelled in a wider sphere than the one he occupies. After first suggesting that Grandet's talents might have propelled him to the forefront of politics, Balzac continues:

Néanmoins, peut-être aussi serait-il également probable que, sorti de Saumur, le bonhomme n'aurait fait qu'une pauvre figure. Peut-être en est-il des esprits comme de certains animaux, qui n'engendrent plus transplantés hors des climats où ils naissent. (GF p. 105)

(Yet, after all, it is equally possible that away from Saumur the worthy cooper would have cut but a poor figure. It may be true that minds, like certain animals, lose their fertility when taken from their native clime.) (P p. 137)

The question of scale is thus raised yet again, and Balzac's comment, after his initial evocation of a potential statesman in Grandet, reduces the old man's undoubted skill as a negotiator to the level of parish craftiness carried to a supreme degree. The question of the supremacy of these wiles is left to the reader to judge, when Grandet's manipulation of his satellites is seen in action over the next few pages. The fact remains that the provincial miser's stratagems do outwit the Parisian creditors.

Further victory for the provinces over Paris is scored when Charles backs an also-ran in the marriage stakes, leaving to M. de Bonfons the triumph of announcing to the worldly-wise adventurer the extent of Eugénie's fortune which he has let slip.

It is evident that Saumur can compete in many ways with Paris, and that Balzac's provincial society provides as valued a perspective on the Restauration as does his evocation of Paris in other novels. What sort of society, then, is represented by Saumur? It has already been noted that Saumur hardly exists as a recognizable town, and that its proximity to Nantes makes it as good a choice as any for Balzac's setting.

Another factor, however, may be that the name of the town has a punning association, a reference to 'saumure' – brine for pickling. This connotation reaches the surface of the novel when Nanon is described, admiringly, as being 'conservée dans de la saumure' (GF p. 168). The town has, in fact, the appearance of a 'ville morte', a conservation area. The early pages, we have seen, insist on the links with the past, and a number of allusions to the characters themselves suggest an artificial preservation. Eugénie at twenty-three is still a child in worldly terms; Nanon at fifty-nine is judged to be capable of bearing children. Eugénie gradually takes on characteristics of both her parents: for example, she cautiously replies in her father's words when shown a letter from M. des Grassins:

– Je vous remercie, dit-elle à Madame des Grassins, *nous verrons cela . . .*
– En ce moment, vous avez toute la voix de défunt votre père, dit Madame des Grassins. (GF p. 183)

('Thank you,' she said; *'we shall see . . .'*
'That sounded exactly like your father!' exclaimed Madame des Grassins.) (P p. 240)

The salon she holds in the years following her father's death is apparently more hospitable than before – we learn of whole clans of Cruchotins! – but Balzac maintains that little has really changed.

Enfin, hormis le nombre des personnages, en remplaçant le loto par le whist, et en supprimant les figures de Monsieur et Madame Grandet, la scène par laquelle commence cette histoire était à peu près la même que par le passé. (GF p. 171)

(In fact, but for the increase in the number of persons present, the substitution of whist for lotto, the absence of Monsieur and Madame Grandet, the scene of this new episode in the story was almost the same as it had been on that first evening long ago.) (P p. 224)

The marriage contracted with de Bonfons also preserves Eugénie as a virgin, just as her life, described in the last pages of the novel, preserves the habits acquired in youth, dressing as her mother once did and following the routines laid down by her father.

Saumur, then, emphasizes the stagnation of provincial life. Balzac also uses geographical references to evoke the pettiness of the provinces in a way that would raise a smile from his Parisian readers. It is a measure of the dullness of the provinces that Eugénie's expectations are spoken of as far away as Angers and Blois:

Que ne disait-on pas d'une héritière dont on parlait à vingt lieues à la ronde, et jusque dans les voitures publiques, d'Angers à Blois inclusivement? (GF p. 37)

(There was little indeed that could be said about an heiress that was left unsaid, when tongues were wagging for fifty miles round, and even in the very public vehicles, from Angers in the west to Blois in the east!) (P p. 47)

Her father's purchase of Froidfond stirred echoes even further off, from Nantes to Orléans, while Eugénie's *coup de théâtre* of 'Restez, monsieur le président'

. . . retentit dans Saumur, de là dans l'arrondissement et dans les quatre préfectures environnantes. (GF p. 183)

(. . . was to create a stir in Saumur and send a wave of excitement from Saumur into the *arrondissement* and the four prefectures round about.) (P pp. 240–41)

Such references to the scale of the action may seem patronizing, as might the local comparison of Grandet to Rothschild, or Balzac's likening of the Cruchot and des Grassins factions to the Medici and Pazzi in Renaissance Florence (GF p. 36, P p. 45). At the same time, the feeling is conveyed that Saumur is a microcosm of wider social conflicts, and of Parisian ones in particular. If *Eugénie Grandet* is compared with *Le Père Goriot*, written a year later, the principle emerges clearly. In both novels, Balzac establishes a historical context reaching back to the Revolution; in both, the possible marriage of an heiress unaware of her prospects forms a part of the plot. In both works, too, we discover that society values money above all things, especially above true love, and yet

69

is impressed by the integrity of those who make sacrifices for love (Eugénie and Mme de Beauséant). Women have become a means of obtaining social standing, either by marriage or by exploiting them in an adulterous relationship. Young men are subjected to temptations, true love struggles against great pressures, society watches and comments. It may be objected that such themes form the staple of novels from Fielding to the present day; yet Balzac's firm placing of events in a particular society inevitably colours these traditional areas of novelistic concern with the image of the epoch. Not for nothing does the action begin in 1819, when Restauration society was beginning to emerge from the débâcle of the imperial adventure. Balzac finds in the new *arriviste* society of the 1820s a brutality but also a vigour which shock and fascinate him. The cult of energy, so close to his personal obsessions and born of the thrusting post-Revolutionary drive of Napoleon's empire, has been turned by military impotence and reactionary politics into an urge to acquire wealth. Grandet's exploitation of historical events predates, of course, the Restauration; but significantly it is in his later years that money is said by Balzac to have become Grandet's 'monomanie'. The upheavals of French society had propelled many from a subservient to a commanding position, with Napoleon standing as the paradigm of this progression. Grandet differs from the national leader in that he does not seek out power or personal glory. Grandet enjoys a position of power without the outer trappings of wealth. His energies are directed towards one purpose only, and, whether stealing marches on rivals in Saumur or dissembling with creditors in Paris, he displays that superior use of his natural gifts and a refusal to disperse his dynamism in social trivia which make him the prototype of capitalism. Eugénie in her turn draws energy from her love, and when the love dies the new forces it has unleashed in her die away, too.

Society, however, consists of ordinary human contacts as well as the greater issues of the day, and in this respect *Eugénie Grandet* provides an incomplete picture. Balzac has chosen to restrict the range of social classes depicted in the novel, just as he has limited the number of actors on his stage. We do not see the house of Mme des Grassins, to sample the delights of refined society, Saumur-style; nor do we visit the poor with Eugénie. When her husband achieves office she divides her life between Saumur and Angers, but we do not follow her. Nanon alone represents the working classes in Saumur. Balzac allows only the war of nerves between Cruchotins and Grassinistes to distract us from the main thrust of his two plots, and even this, of course, is firmly tied to the two principal characters. The claustrophobic atmosphere of *Eugénie Grandet* has, in fact, little to offer as a commentary on 'society' in the more frivolous sense of the word.

11 Classic or Romantic?

How can Balzac's achievement in *Eugénie Grandet* be summed up? Where does the novel stand in the long chain of the masterpieces of French literature? Balzac himself stands at the turning-point of the course of that literature, the transition from the Classical to the new currents of Romanticism which gradually seeped, and then, from about 1825 to 1830, flooded, into French artistic circles. We might expect, therefore, that at least some of his early work would reflect the older tradition, while being the product of the new literature. *Eugénie Grandet* is one such work.

Born in 1799, Balzac was educated in the ethics of the great dramatists and moralists of the Classical age of the seventeenth century, in that cult of restraint and of noble purity of expression so admired in Racine, Corneille, Bossuet and La Fontaine. Literature of a more recent period, too, had upheld these virtues in a modified form. The comedies of Marivaux, and Prévost's novel *Manon Lescaut*, had allowed a certain sensibility to tinge the severe forms of Classicism; by the end of the eighteenth century, Rousseau and others had advanced the claims of a more self-indulgent, less detached approach to emotions such as love, religion, the reaction to nature, in a period which may be called the Pre-Romantic era, but one which was not yet ready to question probingly or to reject outright the long allegiance to the cult of antique values.

Eugénie Grandet finds Balzac upholding some of these values and traditions. To a degree quite remarkable in a novel (as opposed to a play), Balzac observes the unities of theme and of place, though not the unity of time; the number of characters is pared down to a minimum, as in a classical tragedy. His novel begins with an exposition, and thereafter builds to a small number of dramatic climaxes. Even in his use of language, Balzac can achieve miracles of restraint, as in Eugénie's 'Nous verrons cela', which reveals to us the posthumous influence of her father, and, most strikingly, in her 'Restez, monsieur le président'. Moreover, as already noted, the whole sub-genre of the 'roman d'analyse' has strong affinities with Racinian tragedy, and can be traced back to *La Princesse de Clèves*, that masterpiece by Mme de La Fayette.

Against these considerations must be set elements which belong first and foremost to the Romantic school. We note the almost obsessive use of description, an area of the novel in which Balzac was something of a pioneer in French, and which derived directly from Scott, as historical novels by his French contemporaries make clear. Balzac applies such concern with the authenticity of his setting to a contemporary subject, and in doing so asserts at once both the value of realism in the novel and the interest for his contemporaries of a faithful depiction of a society with which the reader would be but imperfectly acquainted. Charles arriving in the Grandets' salon may be as strange as a giraffe to its habitués; but his quizzing scrutiny reveals how far removed both they and their setting are from the concerns of Parisians.

Balzac's handling of his descriptive material often links it directly to the emotions of his characters, notably in the passages concerning the garden. Here his model is Rousseau, but the pathetic fallacy, the projection of human emotions on to nature, was already a commonplace among the earliest French Romantics, such as the poets Lamartine and Hugo. It is also a cliché of the popular fiction of the time, and Pierre Citron has shown, in his Introduction to the Garnier-Flammarion edition of *Eugénie Grandet*, how much this novel owes to the romances of pirates and orphan girls which Balzac wrote under pseudonyms in the 1820s.

From that popular taste for romance and melodrama comes the violence of certain confrontations in *Eugénie Grandet*, and the monomaniac devotion of Grandet and of his daughter to their separate obsessions. The classical restraint of the story-line is thereby undercut and brought into question.

Perhaps most significantly, the *tone* of the work is Romantic. Balzac deploys a range of metaphors and similes which constantly widen the reader's perception of the simple plot, and which direct our sensibilities along paths which Balzac intends us to follow. Thus the frequent religious imagery, overdone though it may occasionally seem to be, emphasizes that area of Eugénie's spirit which the conflicts of the plot tend to submerge, and predispose us to see in her both a victim and a kind of saint.

Balzac departs most radically from the Classical ideal in offering to the reader a constant authorial voice. The imagery referred to above can be seen as a form of this voice, but Balzac often goes beyond the hint, preferring to accost the reader directly and presenting his views for our guidance. Some instances have already been quoted, for example his comments on Nanon (GF pp. 42–3), but one may quote, as a further selection of Balzac's ideas, his observations on the character of the French (GF p. 114), on the difference between men's and women's reactions to crises (GF p. 139), or on the transformations brought about by the approach of death (GF p. 155). Balzac stands as a mediator between the reader and the text, concerned to direct and to interpret. Together with Dickens, he is forging one of the great traditions of the novel in the nineteenth century, one which writers as diverse as Stendhal and Sand, Charlotte Brontë and George Eliot were to pursue, and against which Flaubert and Zola in time reacted.

Eugénie Grandet, then, is a minor work only in terms of length and, perhaps, of scope. Only a year later Balzac was to produce *Le Père Goriot*, a far more complex work in which he discovers, for the first time, the full extent of his aims as a novelist. But *Eugénie Grandet* continues to fascinate and charm, not least because it differs so greatly from the novels to come. Like Jane Austen's *Northanger Abbey* or Mozart's opera *Die Entführung aus dem Serail*, it possesses a youthful charm, a perfection in the marriage of form, content and expression which the artist must regretfully leave behind in order to explore more fully, in greater maturity, his or her chosen field.

Selected Reading

The following works cover a wider spectrum than the present volume, and may usefully be consulted. Some are largely biographical, but others, as their titles indicate, examine Balzac's novels in some detail.

E. Auerbach, *Mimesis*, Doubleday Anchor Books, 1953.

P. Bertault, *Balzac and the Human Comedy*, trans. R. Monges, New York University Press, 1963.

H. J. Hunt, *Honoré de Balzac: a biography*, Athlone Press, 1957.

H. J. Hunt, *Balzac's 'Comédie Humaine'*, Athlone Press, 1959.

S. B. John, in *French Literature and its Background*, ed. J. Cruickshank, Volume 4: *The Early Nineteenth Century*, Oxford University Press, 1969.

H. Levin, *The Gates of Horn*, Oxford University Press, 1966.

F. Marceau, *Balzac and his World*, trans. R. Monges, New York University Press, 1963.

A. Maurois, *Prometheus: the life of Balzac*, trans. N. Denny, Penguin, 1971.

V. S. Pritchett, *Balzac*, Chatto & Windus, 1973.

M. Turnell, *The Novel in France*, Hamish Hamilton, 1950; Penguin, 1962.

FOR THE BEST IN PAPERBACKS, LOOK FOR THE

In every corner of the world, on every subject under the sun, Penguin represents quality and variety – the very best in publishing today.

For complete information about books available from Penguin – including Pelicans, Puffins, Peregrines and Penguin Classics – and how to order them, write to us at the appropriate address below. Please note that for copyright reasons the selection of books varies from country to country.

In the United Kingdom: For a complete list of books available from Penguin in the U.K., please write to *Dept E.P., Penguin Books Ltd, Harmondsworth, Middlesex, UB7 0DA*

In the United States: For a complete list of books available from Penguin in the U.S., please write to *Dept BA, Penguin, 299 Murray Hill Parkway, East Rutherford, New Jersey 07073*

In Canada: For a complete list of books available from Penguin in Canada, please write to *Penguin Books Canada Ltd, 2801 John Street, Markham, Ontario L3R 1B4*

In Australia: For a complete list of books available from Penguin in Australia, please write to the *Marketing Department, Penguin Books Australia Ltd, P.O. Box 257, Ringwood, Victoria 3134*

In New Zealand: For a complete list of books available from Penguin in New Zealand, please write to the *Marketing Department, Penguin Books (NZ) Ltd, Private Bag, Takapuna, Auckland 9*

In India: For a complete list of books available from Penguin, please write to *Penguin Overseas Ltd, 706 Eros Apartments, 56 Nehru Place, New Delhi, 110019*

In Holland: For a complete list of books available from Penguin in Holland, please write to *Penguin Books Nederland B.V., Postbus 195, NL–1380AD Weesp, Netherlands*

In Germany: For a complete list of books available from Penguin, please write to *Penguin Books Ltd, Friedrichstrasse 10 – 12, D–6000 Frankfurt Main 1, Federal Republic of Germany*

In Spain: For a complete list of books available from Penguin in Spain, please write to *Longman Penguin España, Calle San Nicolas 15, E–28013 Madrid, Spain*

PENGUIN CLASSICS

Netochka Nezvanova   Fyodor Dostoyevsky

Dostoyevsky's first book tells the story of 'Nameless Nobody' and introduces many of the themes and issues which will dominate his great masterpieces.

Selections from the Carmina Burana   A verse translation by David Parlett

The famous songs from the *Carmina Burana* (made into an oratorio by Carl Orff) tell of lecherous monks and corrupt clerics, drinkers and gamblers, and the fleeting pleasures of youth.

Fear and Trembling   Søren Kierkegaard

A profound meditation on the nature of faith and submission to God's will which examines with startling originality the story of Abraham and Isaac.

Selected Prose   Charles Lamb

Lamb's famous essays (under the strange pseudonym of Elia) on anything and everything have long been celebrated for their apparently innocent charm; this major new edition allows readers to discover the darker and more interesting aspects of Lamb.

The Picture of Dorian Gray   Oscar Wilde

Wilde's superb and macabre novella, one of his supreme works, is reprinted here with a masterly Introduction and valuable Notes by Peter Ackroyd.

A Treatise of Human Nature   David Hume

A universally acknowledged masterpiece by 'the greatest of all British Philosophers' – A. J. Ayer

A Passage to India   E. M. Forster

Centred on the unresolved mystery in the Marabar Caves, Forster's great work provides the definitive evocation of the British Raj.

The Republic   Plato

The best-known of Plato's dialogues, *The Republic* is also one of the supreme masterpieces of Western philosophy whose influence cannot be overestimated.

The Life of Johnson   James Boswell

Perhaps the finest 'life' ever written, Boswell's *Johnson* captures for all time one of the most colourful and talented figures in English literary history.

Remembrance of Things Past (3 volumes)   Marcel Proust

This revised version by Terence Kilmartin of C. K. Scott Moncrieff's original translation has been universally acclaimed – available for the first time in paperback.

Metamorphoses   Ovid

A golden treasury of myths and legends which has proved a major influence on Western literature.

A Nietzsche Reader   Friedrich Nietzsche

A superb selection from all the major works of one of the greatest thinkers and writers in world literature, translated into clear, modern English.

PENGUIN CLASSICS

Honoré de Balzac	**Cousin Bette**
	Eugénie Grandet
	Lost Illusions
	Old Goriot
	Ursule Mirouet
Benjamin Constant	**Adolphe**
Corneille	**The Cid / Cinna / The Theatrical Illusion**
Alphonse Daudet	**Letters from My Windmill**
René Descartes	**Discourse on Method and Other Writings**
Denis Diderot	**Jacques the Fatalist**
Gustave Flaubert	**Madame Bovary**
	Sentimental Education
	Three Tales
Jean de la Fontaine	**Selected Fables**
Jean Froissart	**The Chronicles**
Théophile Gautier	**Mademoiselle de Maupin**
Edmond and Jules de Goncourt	**Germinie Lacerteux**
J.-K. Huysmans	**Against Nature**
Guy de Maupassant	**Selected Short Stories**
Molière	**The Misanthrope / The Sicilian / Tartuffe / A Doctor in Spite of Himself / The Imaginary Invalid**
Michel de Montaigne	**Essays**
Marguerite de Navarre	**The Heptameron**
Marie de France	**Lais**
Blaise Pascal	**Pensées**
Rabelais	**The Histories of Gargantua and Pantagruel**
Racine	**Iphigenia / Phaedra / Athaliah**
Arthur Rimbaud	**Collected Poems**
Jean-Jacques Rousseau	**The Confessions**
	Reveries of a Solitary Walker
Madame de Sevigné	**Selected Letters**
Voltaire	**Candide**
	Philosophical Dictionary
Émile Zola	**La Bête Humaine**
	Nana
	Thérèse Raquin

FOR THE BEST IN PAPERBACKS, LOOK FOR THE

PENGUIN MASTERSTUDIES

This comprehensive list, designed to help advanced level and first-year undergraduate studies, includes:

SUBJECTS
Applied Mathematics
Biology
Drama: Text into Performance
Geography
Pure Mathematics

LITERATURE
Dr Faustus
Eugénie Grandet
The Great Gatsby
The Mill on the Floss
A Passage to India
Persuasion
Portrait of a Lady
Tender Is the Night
Vanity Fair
The Waste Land

CHAUCER
The Knight's Tale
The Miller's Tale
The Nun's Priest's Tale
The Pardoner's Tale
The Prologue to The Canterbury
 Tales
A Chaucer Handbook

SHAKESPEARE
Hamlet
King Lear
Measure for Measure
Othello
The Tempest
A Shakespeare Handbook

'Standing somewhere between the literal, word-by-word explication of more usual notes and the abstractions of an academic monograph, the Masterstudies series is an admirable introduction to mainstream literary criticism for A Level students, in particular for those contemplating reading English at university. More than that, it is also a model of what student notes can achieve' – *The Times Literary Supplement*